The European Possessions
in the Caribbean Area

AMERICAN GEOGRAPHICAL SOCIETY

MAP OF HISPANIC AMERICA PUBLICATION NO. 4

The European Possessions in the Caribbean Area

A Compilation of Facts Concerning Their Population,
Physical Geography, Resources, Industries, Trade,
Government, and Strategic Importance

BY

RAYE R. PLATT · JOHN K. WRIGHT · JOHN C. WEAVER
American Geographical Society

AND

JOHNSON E. FAIRCHILD
Hunter College, New York

AMERICAN GEOGRAPHICAL SOCIETY

BROADWAY AT 156TH STREET

NEW YORK, N.Y.

1941

CONTENTS

PREFACE

Before the German successes of last spring and summer the American public was little concerned with the island and mainland possessions of Great Britain, France, and the Netherlands in the Caribbean area. Since then countless newspaper and magazine articles have stressed the vital importance of these territories in relation to the security of the Americas: their strategic positions commanding the eastern approaches to the Panama Canal; their potentialities as naval and air bases or as centers of fifth-column activities; their present economic plight; their possible fate in the event of an Axis victory.

This booklet seeks to provide facts concerning the European territorial possessions in the Caribbean area as a basis for an understanding of their condition today and of changes that may occur in the near future. These facts have to do with the relatively permanent elements of physical geography, resources, and population, and also with production, trade, transportation, administration, social conditions, etc. on the eve of the present war. The data have been compiled almost entirely from the reports, periodical articles, and books listed on pp. 101–106. (Mr. Fairchild's section on Martinique is also based in part on field studies carried out on the island in connection with the preparation of a doctoral dissertation for Clark University.) The time that would have been required to complete a more penetrating analysis would have defeated the main purpose, i. e., to bring together in convenient form factual information needed for following the news while the need for such information is still pressing.

The sections on the strategic importance of the Caribbean area and on the British possessions are the work of Mr. Platt, those on the French possessions were contributed by Mr. Fairchild, and those on the Dutch possessions by Dr. Wright with the collaboration of Professor William Van Royen of Brooklyn College, Brooklyn, N. Y. Mr. Weaver contributed the section on the Colombian and Venezuelan islands and collaborated in the preparation of statistical data. The booklet was edited by Dr. Wright.

Grateful acknowledgment is made of the courtesies and help rendered by the Netherlands Consulate and the Netherlands Information Bureau in New York City and especially by Mr. J. Van Stappen, of the latter.

No attempt has been made to provide the booklet with a map of sufficient detail for general reference use. The accompanying map is designed to present facts of strategic importance not found on most maps of the region. For ordinary reference purposes there are the maps of the region in numerous popular-priced atlases. None of these, however, are on a sufficiently large scale to show the islands of the Lesser Antilles in any detail. For those who desire a more detailed map the Caribbean sheets of the American Geographical Society's Map of Hispanic America on the scale of 1 : 1,000,000 are recommended. This is an up-to-date topographical-political map. Topography of the land and the sea floor is shown by contours and hypsometric tints. Towns are classified according to size and administrative importance; railways are classified according to gauge and roads according to character. The map is on a scale large enough—16 miles to the inch—to permit the plotting of information of various sorts in considerable detail. Of the 13 sheets of this map covering the mainland and islands enclosing the Caribbean Sea, 10 have been published and the remaining three—the Habana, Cuba, sheet and two covering the coast of Venezuela—are in various stages of compilation and reproduction. Four additional sheets cover the Guianas. An index map showing the location of the sheets will be sent on request.

Rates of Exchange

In the text of this work values are given in terms of the official currencies of the various colonies and territories: guilders for the Netherlands territories, francs for the French, United States dollars for British Honduras, dollars officially valued at 4s. 10d. for Trinidad and Tobago and for British Guiana, and pounds for the other British colonies. The following table will enable the reader to convert pounds, francs, and guilders for the years 1931–1939 into the approximate values in terms of current United States dollars.

Average Annual Exchange Rates in United States Dollars
(*From Federal Reserve Bulletin*)

Year	Pound	Franc	Guilder
1931	$4.5350	$0.0392	$0.4023
1932	3.5061	0.0393	0.4029
1933	4.2368	0.0503	0.5172
1934	5.0393	0.0657	0.6738
1935	4.9018	0.0660	0.6771
1936	4.9709	0.0611	0.6448
1937	4.9440	0.0405	0.5505
1938	4.8894	0.0288	0.5501
1939	4.4354	0.0251	0.5333

THE BRITISH COLONIES

ADMINISTRATIVE AND ECONOMIC PROBLEMS

The British possessions in the Caribbean area consist of the Central
American colony of British Honduras, the island of Jamaica, and several
groups of smaller islands in the West Indian arc that stretches from Florida
to the mouth of the Orinoco River. With the Bahama Islands at the northern end and Trinidad at the southern, Great Britain holds both ends of
this arc and thus potentially commands two of the most important entrances
to the Caribbean Sea. Because of its proximity to the Caribbean area,
British Guiana, on the South American mainland, is frequently included
in descriptions of the British Caribbean domain and will be thus treated
here.

From the standpoint of administration the possessions of Great Britain
in the Caribbean area comprise colonies of two types—crown colonies
ruled almost exclusively by appointees of the crown with few, if any,
privileges of self-government vested in the people (British Honduras, Leeward Islands, Windward Islands, and Trinidad and Tobago) and colonies
that are partially self-governing by virtue of relatively large elected representation in their local legislative bodies (Bahama Islands, Jamaica and
dependencies, Barbados, and British Guiana). In both types the executive
branch of the government, a Governor and his Executive Council, is appointed by the crown. In the crown colonies the legislative branch, designated as a Legislative Council, consists of official members (that is persons
who are also members of the executive branch of the government) and nonofficial members; the latter usually are appointed or chosen in various
ways but not elected by popular vote, although in some cases a small
minority is elected under limited franchise. In the second type of colony
the legislative branch invariably has a larger elected representation than in
any of the crown colonies and, in most cases, consists of two houses, of
which the upper corresponds to the Legislative Councils of the crown
colonies while the lower is composed of members elected under a franchise
that, although still limited, is more liberal than that of any of the crown
colonies.

Qualifications for electors vary somewhat from colony to colony. The
right to vote is everywhere based chiefly on economic status, although to
some extent recognition is also given to intellectual status as indicated by
certificates or degrees from certain colleges. The required economic status
is in all cases low—ownership of a few dollars worth of real estate or of
personal property of slightly higher value, or payment of a certain small
annual rental—but it is indicative of the low economic level of the great
majority of the people of these colonies that it serves to exclude all but a
small percentage of them from the polls. In Barbados, for example, where
the franchise is comparatively liberal, there were in 1938 only 6381 quali-
fied voters out of a total estimated population of 193,082. Economic quali-

fications for eligibility to election to the legislative assemblies are considerably higher than those for electors. Color, however, plays no part in the required qualifications of either electors or legislators.

There are no direct administrative connections among the British colonies in the Caribbean area, but the Secretary of State for the Colonies in the British Cabinet is ultimately responsible for the administration of their governments, and the Crown Agents appointed by him act as their commercial and financial agents in Great Britain. Various committees and advisory councils have also been set up by the British government to deal with such matters as education, hygiene, agriculture, topographical survey, currency, etc. An Imperial College of Tropical Agriculture established at St. Augustine, Trinidad, in 1921 serves all of the colonies in the Caribbean area by giving undergraduate and postgraduate courses in methods of agriculture and animal husbandry suited to the area and by conducting research projects at a number of well distributed experimental stations. There is also a West Indian Court of Appeal established in 1920 for all the West Indian colonies except Jamaica and consisting of their chief justices.

Because of their adaptability to the production of a wide variety of tropical and subtropical crops and the advantages of their geographical position, it would seem that these British colonies should constitute one of the richest sections of the Empire. The majority of them, however, have had only brief periods of prosperity during the last hundred years, and, even in times of greatest prosperity, economic and social conditions among the masses of the population have usually remained at a very low level. For this the spirit that motivated their early economic development is chiefly to be blamed, but the fact is also generally recognized that the Home Government has been remiss in taking full cognizance of the seriousness of the situation and of the necessity of itself assuming the responsibility for reform. On the North American continent British colonization was largely motivated by a desire to escape intolerable economic conditions or political and religious oppression and the result was the development of a colonial citizenry in which the small landowner predominated. In the Caribbean area, on the other hand, exploitation of agricultural potentialities for large and immediate profits motivated the British colonists, and the great estate, devoted exclusively to sugar growing with slave labor, almost completely eliminated the small white landowner or tenant and also largely precluded the cultivation of food crops for local consumption.

The abolition of slavery (in 1834 on Antigua and in 1836 elsewhere) is often said to have been the first serious blow to the sugar industry, but the industry was already on the decline before emancipation as the result of a number of factors, notably the increasing practice of absentee landlordism and changes in the demands and supplies of the world market. Evidence that lack of an adequate and readily available supply of labor resulting from emancipation was not the real cause of the decline is to be found in the fact that where indentured East Indian labor was introduced it served to relieve the situation only partially. A very real blow was struck the industry, however, when in the 1880's the free trade policy of the British government was extended to include sugar. With their monopoly of the sugar market in the United Kingdom and the other British possessions gone, the sugar growers of the British Caribbean possessions were in the impossible position of having to compete with the subsidized beet-sugar industry of the European continent. So widespread was the resulting collapse of the industry and so serious the situation of the laboring population that the British government in 1897 set up a Royal Commission to inquire into the causes of the disaster and recommend measures for relief.

The recommendations led to the present variations in the legislative and administrative organization of the several colonies. Changes were adopted in an attempt to adjust the balance between local self-government and Home Government to each colony's peculiar needs and capabilities. Also, in accordance with the recommendations of the Commission serious efforts were made to dispel some of the disadvantages of monoculture by introducing or increasing the cultivation of other crops, such as cacao, cotton, citrus fruits, bananas, and coconuts, and to lower the cost of sugar production by introducing more productive strains of cane, improving methods of cultivation, and setting up local refineries.

Quite apart from whatever might have been accomplished in the way of permanent relief by the measures recommended by the Royal Commission, a number of factors combined during the second half of the first quarter of the present century to give the colonies a brief period of comparative prosperity. One was the demand for labor in the construction of the Panama Canal and on the banana plantations of Central America and the sugar plantations of Cuba and the Dominican Republic; another, the market for the agricultural products of the colonies, particularly sugar, created by the World War. Unfortunately the temporary character of this prosperity was not recognized, and consequently the opportunity to effect permanent improvements at a time when funds would have been available was in most cases missed. Both directly and indirectly the general economic depression brought suffering to the colonies. It not only produced a disastrous effect on the market for their agricultural products but led to the return of large labor forces which for some years had been finding agricultural employment in Central America, Cuba, and the Dominican Republic. These more recent repatriates augmented the many who had returned after the completion of the Panama Canal and whose effect on the labor market was first seriously felt with the fall of the market for agricultural products after the World War. Not only have these returned laborers themselves increased the labor supply, but large numbers whom they had supported by remittances from abroad found themselves in the position of having to try to earn their own living.

Added to these effects of the depression has been an increasing incidence of diseases affecting almost all of the exportable crops and occurring at a time when the colonies have not been in a financial position to combat them effectively—mosaic disease in sugar cane, Panama disease and spot leaf in bananas, witch broom in cacao. Coffee, citrus fruits, and coconuts have also suffered, and even Jamaica's special crop, pimento, the world's only source of allspice, has been almost wiped out by rust.

To be mentioned also is the progressive effect as shipping has changed from sail to coal to fuel oil. No little of the prosperity of the island colonies in the days of sailing ships was due to the need of numerous harbors for protection from hurricanes as well as for revictualing, and the selection of harbors and town sites throughout the islands was dictated to a large extent by the demands of sail transportation. Although use of coal greatly diminished the importance of these ports, the necessity for conveniently located coaling stations remained as long as coal was the chief fuel. Today the use of oil for fuel as well as the development of refrigeration for food supplies has all but completed the process of obsolescence. The present system of trade agreements and preferential tariffs within the British Commonwealth and more particularly the separate trade agreements and improved shipping arrangements entered into between Canada and the various Caribbean colonies in 1925 have served effectively to ward off the complete disaster that might have resulted from the world economic depression. Nevertheless, the problem of unemployment has recently become so acute that the Colonial Office instituted two separate investigations in 1938. Many of the recommendations of the two commissions which carried out these investigations were accepted for immediate action. The reports indicate the deplorable social conditions throughout the Caribbean colonies and recognize that improvement must be chiefly the responsibility of the Home Government.[1]

BAHAMA ISLANDS

Government. Executive branch: Governor and Executive Council (not more than 9 members) appointed by the crown. Legislative branch: Governor, Legislative Council appointed by the crown, Representative Assembly (29 members) elected under limited franchise.

PHYSICAL FEATURES

The Bahama Islands consist of about 20 inhabited islands and more than 3000 islets, cays, and rocks. The land area of the 19 principal islands, of which Andros (1600 sq. mi.) is the largest, is about 4375 square miles. The Turks and Caicos Islands, which form the southeast end of the archipelago, were formerly administered as a part of the Bahama Colony but are now governed as dependencies of Jamaica.

[1]West Indian Royal Commission, 1938–39, Recommendations presented by the Secretary of state for the colonies to Parliament by command of His Majesty, February, 1940. Labour conditions in the West Indies. Report by Major G. St. J. Orde Browne, O. B. E. Presented by the Secretary of state in the colonies to Parliament by command of His Majesty, July, 1939.

Geologically and physiographically the Bahamas are related to Florida and the Florida keys. They are formed largely of minute particles of calcareous sand derived from shells. Originally piled up by wind action into low, rounded hills and ridges on a shallow marine platform, these sands have been consolidated by exposure into rock that on the surface is as hard as flint but underneath is soft enough to be easily sawed into building blocks. The hills and ridges nowhere exceed 100 to 200 feet in height except on Cat Island, where they rise to nearly 400 feet.

One of the most arresting aspects of the islands is the almost complete lack of normal stream-erosion features. Instead, there are typical karst forms produced by the action of rain water on highly soluble rock—pot-holes, boiling holes, peculiar cylindrical "banana holes" reaching to depths as great as 40 feet, and cavities and caverns, many of which have subterranean connection with the sea. Because of the lack of streams or other fresh-water bodies, man and beast depend largely on rain water collected in cisterns, although a few natural and dug wells also supply drinkable water.

As the result of a geologically recent subsidence estimated at about 300 feet, much of the far more extensive land surface of former times now consists of shallow submerged banks above which rise many coral heads and reefs. The barrier reefs along the exposed eastern border of the outer rim of islands are so extensive as to make this shore almost inaccessible to shipping. Numerous channels separate the islands into groups. Although some are of sufficient depth to afford through passage to ships of deep draft and the principal passages are well lighted, most of the channels are difficult of navigation.

CLIMATE AND VEGETATION

The Bahamas have a typically subtropical oceanic climate. The mean annual temperature at Nassau is 77.2° F., with the mean temperature for the warmest month (August) 83° F. and for the coolest month (January) 71.7° F. Because of the warming effect of the Gulf Stream, the islands have an advantage over near-by Florida, which occasionally suffers damaging frosts; the lowest temperature recorded for the Bahamas is 51.5° F. (January, 1905). The average annual rainfall is about 46 inches, but in 1938 only 28.91 inches were recorded on New Providence. The rainy season is from June to October, with little rain during the rest of the year. West Indian hurricanes of destructive force visit the islands on an average of about five times in every ten years.

From the sea the islands appear as low stretches of green bordered by bands of white beach or surf. Where there is a cover of soil on the rocks it is usually very fertile, although thin. In places, as on New Providence, such areas are frequently overgrown with pines like the pines of the Florida coast and are called "pine barrens." Only a few of the islands are forested. Andros and the Abaco Islands, however, have good growths of mahogany, lignum vitae, mastic, ironwood, and bulletwood. The natural

vegetation of most of the islands is a stunted growth, with mangrove pre-
dominating. On the flat lands there are some savana areas, but low thickets
are of more frequent occurrence.

HISTORICAL NOTE

Although Columbus made his first American landfall in the Bahamas,
the Spanish seem never to have settled there. Settlements were established
by Englishmen from Bermuda on Eleuthera in 1646 and on New Providence
in 1666. The history of the archipelago has always centered around New
Providence Island, which has the best harbor (Nassau). The islands were
long used as a retreat for pirates and buccaneers, whose depredations became so serious a menace to Britain's trade with her North American and
Caribbean colonies that a crown governor was sent out with a garrison
in 1718. With the outbreak of the American Revolution, loyalists from
the southern colonies of North America sought refuge in the Bahamas,
many of them people of substance who brought money and slaves. Cotton
cultivation was introduced and large areas planted—nearly 4000 acres on
Long Island by 1783—only to be almost completely abandoned before
1800 because of the destructive inroads of insect pests.

The islands came into prominence during the Civil War in the United
States when Nassau was the center of the blockade-running trade with the
Confederate States.

POPULATION

Of the present population, estimated as 67,720 in 1938, the majority
are colored, but the proportion of whites (about one-sixth) is rather higher than that in most of the other Caribbean colonies of Great Britain. New
Providence Island, with about 20,000 inhabitants on an area of only 60
square miles, has a little less than a third of the total population, and
Nassau, on this island, with a population of about 17,000, is the capital of
the colony and its only large town. On Great Abaco Island, with a population of 4233 in 1931, whites predominate, descendants largely of loyalists
from the revolting North American colonies. The inhabitants of Cat
Island (population 3959 in 1931) are also chiefly of loyalist ancestry, and,
indeed, a large fraction of the colored population of the whole colony is
said to be descended from the slaves brought by the loyalists. The inhabitants of the small, densely populated Harbor Island, off the northeast
coast of Eleuthera, are mainly descendants of the buccaneers and have a
communal land system dating from buccaneer times. English is universally
spoken.

STANDARD OF LIVING

The standard of living, particularly the housing, is decidedly higher than
in the other British colonies in the Caribbean area, in spite of the fact that
living costs are greater. There is comparative freedom from tropical

disease. Syphilis, tuberculosis, and pellagra are the principal diseases, and it is believed that the first is the cause of the present surprisingly high infant mortality (212.5 per 1000 living births for the whole colony). The diet of the laboring class is also fairly good as compared with the other colonies. Most of the food is produced locally, although here, as elsewhere in the Caribbean area, imported polished rice and white flour are popular and vegetables little used, except yams and sweet potatoes. The sponge, tortoise-shell, and pearl-shell industries and agriculture furnished the principal markets for labor until the development of the winter tourist trade from the United States. Now large numbers from the so-called Out Islands are attracted to New Providence during the tourist season, and, although the work is seasonal, wages are good and gratuities liberal. Since enough work is provided by agriculture and fishing in the Out Islands during the slack season, unemployment is not a serious problem.

Production and Trade

For many years the collecting and preparation of sponges for the market and the collecting of tortoise and pearl shells were the chief industries. The sponge industry, always by far the most important, suffered severely during the world economic depression, with exports falling from £109,203 in 1927 to £58,350 in 1934; by 1938 it had made a temporary recovery, with exports amounting to £90,054, but it is now reported that the sponge beds have recently suffered severely from disease and that the industry has been brought almost to a standstill. Unless this is checked, its effect on the economic life of the colony will be most disastrous, since about 12 per cent of the inhabitants are engaged in the industry. Sisal was an important product for a number of years and developed rapidly until 1925, when the acreage planted to this crop was 16,000 and the export value £252,419, as compared with £51,329 in 1920. Since 1925, however, production has progressively decreased owing to competition rapidly developing elsewhere and to the general decline of the world market. By 1938 the acreage was only 3204 and the export value only £1,275.

With the failure of the sponge and sisal crops, tomatoes have now become the leading and, in fact, the only important export crop (£92,497 in 1927; £20,444 in 1934; £25,366 in 1938), since the exportation of lumber and shell, which for a number of years held third and fourth places in the colony's exports, has also greatly diminished. Exports of tomatoes also fell off badly when import duties practically closed the United States market to them, but they are on the increase now as the result of a growing Canadian demand.

The economic situation, however, is by no means so serious as would appear from the figures, since the winter tourist trade from the United States is now really the mainstay of the colony. No data are available on the precise amount of money that the tourists bring annually to New Providence, but it is estimated at not less than £1,000,000. An important part of this money is spent in local shops stocking high-grade British goods, particularly articles of clothing.

TRANSPORTATION AND COMMUNICATIONS

From a strategic standpoint the Bahamas command two of the important trade routes to the Caribbean area and the Panama Canal: the route from the United States and Canada through the Crooked Island Passage and thence into the Windward Passage between Cuba and Haiti and the route through Caicos Passage, by which ships from Europe enter the Windward Passage. In normal times, however, the islands are of little consequence in world sea-borne transportation, although locally well served with shipping. There is a direct monthly passenger service (14 days) and freight service between Great Britain and Nassau as well as a fast fortnightly passenger and freight service (3 days) between New York and Nassau. Nassau is also a port of call for Canadian steamships on a regular fortnightly run between Montreal or Halifax and Kingston, Jamaica. During the summer months (May to December, inclusive) a weekly mail, passenger, and freight service is operated between Miami and Nassau, and, this service is stepped up to twice a week in January and April and to three times a week at the height of the tourist season in February and March. Air service for passengers and mail is on a daily schedule between these two ports during the winter months and on a thrice-a-week schedule in summer. The only port other than Nassau where there is any shipping is that of Mathew Town on Great Inagua Island; here in normal times ships of a Netherlands line call principally to take on stevedores for work on cargoes at South American ports. Transportation among the islands is by motor boats or sailing vessels. There are no railroads on any of the islands and few good roads except on New Providence and Eleuthera.

The close connection of the Bahamas with the United States is particularly well shown in the routing of telegraphic communications between the Bahamas and the outside world. Formerly this was by way of a cable between Nassau and Miami laid down in 1892, but this cable has now been abandoned in favor of 24-hour radiotelegraph service with all parts of the world, also by way of Miami. A similar service is maintained through the radiotelegraph station at Kingston, Jamaica, and directly with ships at sea. All the more important islands of the group are connected with Nassau by radiotelegraph and there is radiotelephone service between Nassau and a few of the islands and between Nassau and a number of points in various parts of the world.

HARBORS AND SEAPLANE BASES

Only Nassau Harbor can accommodate ships of more than nine-foot draft. This harbor is 200 yards wide at its entrance (at the west end) but narrows to barely 100 yards before it leads to the turning basin which forms the harbor proper. The outer part of the channel has a depth of 27 feet, and the inner 25 feet, while the greater part of the turning basin is also 25 feet deep.

There are established seaplane anchorages in Nassau Harbor, at West End Settlement on Great Bahama Island, and at Cat Island on the outer rim of the archipelago, although none of these have facilities for large-scale operations. Emergency seaplane anchorages with still more limited facilities are found at North Bimini Harbor, in the Great Lake on Watling Island, and in the lagoon on Conception Island. No established landing field is in service at present, but a combined government and commercial field is under construction (1940) two miles south-southeast of Nassau.

JAMAICA AND DEPENDENCIES (CAYMAN ISLANDS, TURKS AND CAICOS ISLANDS, MORANT AND PEDRO CAYS)

Government. Executive branch: Governor and Privy Council appointed by the crown or provisionally nominated by the Governor. Legislative branch: Legislative Council consisting of the Governor and three other official members, not more than 10 persons appointed by the crown or provisionally nominated by the Governor, and 14 persons (one for each parish of the island) elected under limited franchise.

The dependencies of Turks and Caicos Islands and the Cayman Islands are directly subject to the Governor of Jamaica; for each of them he appoints a Commissioner. The Cayman Islands have a local Legislative Assembly consisting of justices of the peace appointed by the Governor and vestrymen elected locally. Turks and Caicos have a Legislative Board consisting of the Commissioner, a judge, and not fewer than two nor more than four persons appointed by the Governor.

PHYSICAL FEATURES

With an area of about 4450 square miles, Jamaica is third in size of the Greater Antilles group of the West Indies (Cuba, Hispaniola, Jamaica, and Puerto Rico). In general aspect it closely resembles the other islands of the Greater Antilles, with its wooded mountains, limestone plateaus, and steep seaward slopes rising abruptly from a coastal plain that in most places is extremely narrow. The Blue Mountains (maximum elevation 7388 feet), which begin near the east end of the island and parallel the northeast coast for about a third of its length, are the worn-down core of an ancient range, once much more extensive. Over the western two-thirds of the island and partly encircling the Blue Mountains is a plateau of white limestone arching gently down north and south to the sea. Another ancient core brought to light by erosion of this plateau forms several small chains (maximum elevation 3165 feet) with deeply cut flanks that parallel the axis of the Blue Mountains.

From the sea the island appears to be ruggedly mountainous, but its most characteristic feature is the karst forms produced by the action of tropical rain on the highly soluble limestone of the plateau—sinks enclosed by steep walls and separated by roughly serrated ridges, deep canyons through which flow abundant streams, and subterranean water courses. The larger sinks form great basin-shaped valleys. Some of these have no outlets or only subterranean drainage; others are drained to the sea by streams that have broken through their walls; and still others merge with the coastal plains. Protected by their walls, with copious streams for irrigation and for turning mill wheels in the days before steam was used, these large valleys and a number of the smaller ones are ideal for tropical and subtropical agriculture, and in them are found the plantations and the greatest densities of population.

Most of the rivers are not navigable, but several on the south side (Black, Salt, and Cabaritta, the most important) are navigable for barges for some distance (Black River for 30 miles) and are much used for bringing produce down to the sea. Living coral surrounds the western part of the island in an almost uninterrupted band, and coral heads covered with mangrove occur in Montego Bay and some of the bays at the southeast end of the island.

CLIMATE

Because of its varied topography, Jamaica has a variety of climates, but they are generally agreeable and healthful. At Kingston, in one of the hottest and driest parts of the island, the mean annual temperature is 78.7° F., with the mean temperature for the hottest month (July) 81.4° F. and for the coolest month (February) 75.7° F. The highest temperature recorded at Kingston is 97.8° F. (August, 1923), and the lowest 56.7° F. (December, 1887). The more densely inhabited areas lie mostly between 1000 and 3000 feet, where the mean annual temperature varies between 75.7° F. and 68.7° F., according to the elevation. The south side of the island receives less rain than the north side, the driest sections being those shut off by the Blue Mountains from the northeasterly winds (annual mean at Kingston, 32.6 inches). On the plateau the rainfall is much higher, reaching 100 inches on the summit of the limestone plateau and 208 inches at Moore Town on the northeast side of the Blue Mountains. Heavy morning mists are characteristic of many of the interior valleys, making them particularly favorable for sugar cane and bananas. The rainy season is from May to October, and, although there is no record of a completely rainless month, the recorded rainfall for the island has fallen as low as .48 inches in February, the driest month.

VEGETATION

The varied climate and topography of Jamaica is reflected in the great variety of its natural vegetation. Most of the forests that originally covered all but the steeper ridges and crests of the mountains and the arid sections on the south side have been cut, but, except where kept down by cultivation and pasturage, second-growth forests containing much valuable timber have taken their place. This includes such cabinet woods as mahogany, rosewood, sandalwood, lignum vitae, and ebony. Lancewood for ship spars and various hardwoods suitable for railway ties are still cut in large quantities.

Logwood, which quickly grows up in abandoned fields, and fustic are still exported in considerable quantities. Bamboo, numerous varieties of palms, and tree ferns are characteristic of the northeast section of the island where the rainfall is heaviest. In the western part, the forests are largely open and carpeted with grass. Here the pimento or allspice tree occurs in large numbers. On the drier south side, especially in the broad coastal plains like that of Liguanea on which Kingston stands, the natural vegetation is chiefly xerophytic with many varieties of thorny acacias, including mesquite and cactus.

HISTORICAL NOTE

Jamaica was discovered by Columbus in 1494, and the first settlement was made on St. Ann's Bay in 1509 under the direction of his son, Diego. Although attacked by the British in 1596 and again in 1643, the island remained in Spanish possession until 1655, when it was taken by a British force sent out by Cromwell against Hispaniola. British title to the island was recognized by the Treaty of Madrid in 1670, but a civil government set up under a constitution granted by Charles II had already been established in 1661.

The rapid early growth of the colony in British hands was due to the wealth brought in by the buccaneers, who made Port Royal their headquarters and storehouse. When the Royal African Company was formed in 1672 and given the monopoly of the slave trade, Jamaica at once became one of the world's most important slave markets. Sugar growing was introduced about this time. In 1807, the year of the abolition of the slave trade, there were 319,821 slaves in the colony, 86,821 of whom had been imported during the last eight years of the trade.

Under the original constitution of 1661 the government consisted of a Governor and Executive Council appointed by the crown and an elected Legislative Assembly, but after the suppression of a serious rebellion of the colored population in 1865 it was felt that a constitution giving greater control to the British government was needed. At first a government completely appointive by the crown was established, but, by Orders in Council in 1884 and Amending Orders in 1895, the present form of government was established, with a Legislative Council composed partly of elected representatives.

POPULATION

Jamaica, with an estimated population of 1,173,645 at the end of 1938 (density, 267 to the square mile) has nearly half the population of the British colonies in the Caribbean area. Kingston, its capital, with a population (including Port Royal) of about 115,000, is the largest city in these colonies,[2] Port of Spain, Trinidad, with 89,550, being second, and George-

[2]Other important towns according to the 1921 census (no later estimates are available) are: Spanish Town (8694), Port Antonio (6272), Montego Bay (6580), Savanna la Mar (3442), Port Maria (2481), St. Ann's Bay (2090), Falmouth (2136).

town, British Guiana, with 67,584, third. English is universally spoken in Jamaica.

Less than 2 per cent of the population are white, about 18 per cent are of mixed white and Negro blood, and about three-fourths are counted as pure Negro. There are also some 20,000 East Indians (slightly more than 2 per cent), as well as about 4000 Chinese. The East Indians are either former indentured laborers, brought in to work on the sugar plantations after the slaves were freed, or their descendants (36,584 were brought in between 1845 and 1916, and 15,305 returned to India at the end of their indenture). Some of the earliest immigrants were Spanish Jews who had been deported to Central America by the Inquisition but settled finally at Port Royal to trade in Spanish booty brought in by the buccaneers. Their descendants are said to "form today a valuable and influential element in the island society."[3]

Subsistence Farming

Further advances in subsistence farming have been made in Jamaica than in any of the other British colonies in the Caribbean area. The descendants of the former slaves have a land-holding instinct derived from a master-slave economy that was peculiar to Jamaica. On the sugar estates there was plenty of land not suitable for cane, and hence the slaves were not only required to grow their own food but were even encouraged to sell their surplus. This relieved the masters of all responsibility for maintaining their slaves—a situation quite different from that on Barbados, for instance, where most of the land was so valuable for cane growing that it could not be spared for food crops and consequently the masters in general had to provide all maintenance for the slaves. The eagerness of the freed Jamaican slave to acquire land was, therefore, due to the fact the he had had no experience in the matter of obtaining food except by growing it and no experience in obtaining his other necessities except by selling his surplus. He thus had a subsistence-farming tradition that prevails in his descendants today.

The total area of Jamaica is about 2,848,160 acres. The Collector General's report for 1930 shows that 2,446,960 acres were included in 213,395 privately owned holdings and that about half of these (108,447), comprising 352,550 acres, were in plots of one-half an acre to five acres. These small plots were providing some part, and in a great many cases a substantial part, of the living of half the families of the island. Another one-sixth of the population were obtaining a "comfortable independence" on 31,038 holdings, totaling 519,908 acres, in parcels of five to fifty acres. The number of small holdings is steadily increasing as the result of a general policy pursued by the colonial government for many years. In 1939 £500,000 were appropriated to speed up the process as a remedy for unemployment, which has become an acute problem in the colony in recent

[3]Olivier, S. H. O.: Jamaica, the blessed island, London [1936], p. 14.

years and culminated in serious strikes and riots in the spring of that year. It would seem that there is land available for considerable further subsistence-farm settlement, since more than half of the privately owned land (1,368,465 acres) in 1930 was divided into only 1391 parcels, averaging 1000 acres, and a large part of these were not being worked economically or profitably by their owners.

LABOR AND UNEMPLOYMENT

The only manufacturing of any account carried on in Jamaica, other than sugar refining and rum distilling, is the making of cigars and cigarettes, the local demand for which is now practically all supplied by local products, and some manufacturing of lard substitutes and soaps from coconut oil. The tourist trade, though promising, is still in its infancy. Agriculture and the services connected with exporting its products are, therefore, the only local markets for labor on any large scale. Wages are low, running from 2s. to 3s. a day for ordinary unskilled labor to 4s. to 9s. for certain forms of skilled labor, artisans, and foremen. Much of the planting, cultivating, and harvesting on the estates is piece work at equally low rates. The cost of living for town dwellers of the working class averages 11s. to 17s. a week, so that the margin is very small even with continuous employment, whereas much of the work is seasonal. The situation of the worker on the estates is better. If he must pay rent, it is much lower than in the towns; food is cheaper, and a considerable amount can be collected from wild or semiwild trees such as breadfruit, mangoes, coconuts; and frequently livestock (poultry, goats, etc.) can be kept.

The present problem of unemployment is due to several causes. The world economic depression seriously affected the market for the island's exports. Disease has greatly reduced the production of some crops—cane, bananas, coconuts, coffee, and citrus fruits—and even Jamaica's own peculiar product, the pimento tree (the world's only source of allspice), has been almost completely destroyed by rust. The small farmer who has depended on one or more of these for his cash crop is particularly hard hit because he cannot undertake the spraying and other measures necessary to combat the diseases. In addition, the depression has practically stopped the demand for agricultural and construction labor in Central America, Cuba, and the Dominican Republic, which for many years afforded an important outlet for Jamaican labor, the average annual exodus from 1883 to 1935 being about 10,000, and the average annual remittances about £125,000. No little blame must also be put on the lure of the town. In 1938 from 12,000 to 14,000 were reported unemployed in Kingston and St. Andrew (no estimates are available for the rest of the colony).

DIET

Although there is little menace of actual starvation on the island even under most serious conditions of unemployment, the diet of the laboring class, as distinguished from the small proprietors, is at all times too largely farinaceous to be of satisfactory nutritional value. The average annual slaughter of cattle raised locally is only about 33,000 head. No figures are available on the consumption of locally grown pork, but there must be an appreciable consumption of goat meat, since 231,000 goatskins were exported in 1936. Fish of excellent quality may be had in the coastal districts, but little of it finds its way inland in either fresh or salted form. Out of food imports valued at £1,145,928 in 1936, £493,744 went for salt fish, canned milk, meat, butter, and butter substitutes (the remainder was spent for grain, flour, and dried beans and peas), but this amount suggests a relatively small per capita consumption of these foods when distributed among a population of 1,173,645.

PRODUCTION AND TRADE

Jamaica's production for export is exclusively agricultural. Sugar was the chief export crop from the introduction of cane in 1672 to the end of the nineteenth century, in spite of the fact that in Jamaica the industry suffered more severely from the effects of slave emancipation than in any of the other British colonies in the Caribbean area and had more or less progressively declined for the past hundred years. Bananas have been the chief export crop since the early years of the present century. The enormous banana trade from the Caribbean area and northern South America to the United States, Canada, and Europe began in 1867 when an American trading schooner carried the first shipment from Jamaica to the Boston market. The industry grew so rapidly that in 1896 the crop held third place among the export crops of the island—exceeded only by sugar and coffee. The producing acreage that year was: sugar, 30,036; coffee, 25,559; bananas, 19,227. By 1899, however, the producing acreage in each of these three crops was about equal—approximately 25,000 acres—and from that time on bananas have gained more or less steadily on the other agricultural products until their export value now is 50 to 60 per cent of that of the total exports of the island. The acreage in coffee meanwhile has fallen from 25,902 in 1899 to 6265 in 1939. The future of Jamaican agricultural production for export depends both on the recovery of the world market and on the success of measures to combat the diseases that are now menacing all the export crops and have nearly wiped out the pimento tree.

The principal exports in 1938 in the order of their value were: bananas, £2,916,956; sugar, £859,500; rum, £247,892; pimento (allspice), £207,-070; grapefruit and oranges, £135,393; coffee, £132,907; coconuts, £83,155; ginger, £50,939; logwood extract, £50,677; cacao, £47,020; honey, £18,049; cigars, £17,028; logwood, £14,239. As the result of preferential duties almost the whole of the banana crop now goes to Great Britain. Eighty-five per cent of the sugar and rum goes to Canada, and most of the remainder to Great Britain, which also takes 90 per cent of the ginger. The bulk of the coffee goes to the United States,

except for the celebrated Blue Mountain product, considered by many experts the finest in the world. This goes almost entirely to Great Britain, but represents only 2½ per cent of the total crop. The cacao is practically all taken by Canada. The figure for coconut export represents only about half the crop, the other half being used for the local manufacture of edible oils, lard compounds, and soap for local consumption.

Transportation and Communications

Mention has already been made of the importance of the harbor at Kingston in buccaneer times and later as the center of the Caribbean slave trade. In the days of coal-burning steamers the fueling station there was one of the most important in the Caribbean area and Kingston was a regular port of call for revictualing, particularly for steamships with goods and passengers for Central American ports or for transshipment to the west coast by way of the Panama Railway. Today, with oil the principal steamship fuel and refrigeration in universal use, Kingston has lost much of its former importance as a port of call, and in spite of its proximity to the Windward Passage route to the Panama Canal, steamers from the United States or European ports en route for ports beyond the canal usually do not stop there. In normal times, however, the port was well served by direct passenger lines from Great Britain (12 to 14 days), by direct British freight lines, and by several British, Netherlands, and German lines engaged in the Caribbean trade. Steamship lines connected with American fruit companies afford passenger and freight service between the United States and Jamaica and between Jamaica and the Central American countries. The Canadian National Line has regular fortnightly sailings between Montreal or Halifax and Kingston by way of Bermuda and Nassau. The regular twice-a-week passenger, mail, and freight air service of the Pan American Airways between New York and South America has a stop at Kingston, and the same company provides a weekly service between Kingston and Trinidad via Haiti, Puerto Rico, and various islands of the Lesser Antilles.

Fruit-company and other steamship lines maintain coastwise service by motor or sailing vessels when cargo is available. The island is served internally by a railway system totaling 210 miles, which connects Kingston by a cross-country route with Montego Bay, the island's second port, on the northwest coast, and with Annotto Bay and Port Antonio, on the northeast coast. There are also two short branch lines into the interior. Jamaica's road system is excellent, with 2458 miles of good roads (largely metaled or tarred) and some 4438 miles of so-called parochial roads, connecting all but the rougher parts of the interior with a close network.

There are submarine cable connections with New York, with Montreal and London via Halifax, and with Turks Island, Bermuda, Barbados, Santiago, Havana, and Suan Juan and Ponce (Puerto Rico); also a radiotelegraph station with world-wide connections at Kingston, and radiotelephone connections by way of Miami. The island itself is served with a fairly well distributed telegraph and telephone system.

HARBORS AND SEAPLANE BASES

Its central location with respect to the whole Caribbean area, its relatively large area, and its good harbors combine to make Jamaica, from a strategic point of view, one of the most important, if not the most important, of the European colonies in the Caribbean area.

Kingston Harbor is a lagoon about ten miles long by two broad and is protected from the sea by a long, narrow spit called the Palisadoes. The entrance channel is narrow and tortuous and demands careful piloting, but approximately 7 square miles of the habor have a depth of from 7 to 10 fathoms. The harbor is fortified, although it is doubtful if it could be considered really well fortified against present-day attack armament, and has long been the main base of the British fleet in the Caribbean.

Other ports capable of accommodating ships of considerable draft are, on the north coast, Port Antonio (controlling depth 42 feet, railway pier with 19 to 26 feet of water), St. Ann's Bay (deep-water anchorage—6 to 7 fathoms—small, but ample room for small craft), Montego Bay (outer anchorage 40 fathoms, inner anchorage 6 to 9 fathoms, two railway piers but with only shallow water), and Lucea (small but good, 5 to 5¾ fathoms in anchorage). On the south side are Morant Bay (4 to 6 fathoms in anchorage, 4 piers with 18-foot depths), Black River (4 to 4½ fathoms in anchorage, several wharves with cranes), and Savanna la Mar (3¼ to 4½ fathoms in anchorage, several wharves, some of which have cranes).

The many harbors of Jamaica, large and small, afford numerous possibilities for the development of seaplane bases. There is an established seaplane base at the southeast end of Kingston Harbor with depths of 4 to 48 feet and with radio direction finder, dock, and facilities for servicing, although repair facilities are limited at present. Emergency seaplane anchorages but no repair facilities are available at Port Antonio, Montego Bay, and Port Morant. There are no landing fields on the island, although one is now under construction on the Palisadoes near Kingston.

LEEWARD ISLANDS OF GREAT BRITAIN

Government. The Leeward Islands Colony of Great Britain is a quasi-federation consisting of four presidencies: Antigua (with its dependencies, Barbuda and Redonda), St. Christopher (St. Kitts) and Nevis (with Anguilla and Sombrero), Montserrat, and the Virgin Islands. Executive branch: Governor and Executive Council appointed by the crown. Legislative branch: Legislative Council consisting of ten official members, seven elected members (three each chosen from their Councils by the nonofficial members of the Legislative Councils of Antigua and St. Christopher-Nevis, and one by those of the Legislative Council of Montserrat), and one member nominated by the Governor for the Virgin Islands Presidency, which has no legislature. St. Christopher-Nevis Presidency and Antigua have appointed Administrators, Montserrat and the Virgin Islands appointed Commissioners. All have appointed Executive Councils, and all except the Virgin Islands have partly appointed and partly elected Legislative Councils.

PHYSICAL FEATURES

The Leeward Islands Colony consists of two main clusters of islands separated from one another by the 30-mile-wide Anegada Passage. Northwest of the passage lie the British Virgin Islands, comprising about 32 islands and rocks. Southeast of the passage the three presidencies of Antigua, St. Christopher and Nevis (with their dependency Anguilla), and Montserrat form a fairly compact group, except for Anguilla, lying about 55 miles north of St. Christopher, beyond intervening French and Dutch islands. The small, rocky Sombrero, some 35 miles northeast of Anguilla, belongs to the Virgin Islands presidency, from which, however, it is separated by Anegada Passage.

The Virgin Islands are of the same general geological composition as the Greater Antilles: a foundation of ancient crystalline rock has been deeply overlaid with conglomerates and clays, having an outer mantle of marine limestones and fringed with coral reefs. Tortola and Virgin Gorda, two of the three largest of the British islands of the group, are rugged, barren mountain crests (Tortola rising to 1780 feet, Virgin Gorda to 1370), poorly watered and largely rough waste land. Anegada, at the extreme northeast corner of the group, is very low, with no elevation above 30 feet.

The Lesser Antilles from Anegada Passage to the passage between Grenada and Trinidad consist primarily of a curving line of high volcanic islands. In the Leeward Islands northward from Guadeloupe, this line is bordered on the outer, or Atlantic, side by more or less scattered groups of lower islands. Both the inner and the outer islands rest on the same ancient volcanic basement. On the outer islands, the basement is deeply overlaid with white calcareous rocks, mostly limestones, but on the inner chain these deposits have been obliterated by subsequent volcanic eruptions or had already been eroded away before the eruptions took place.

The inner volcanic islands are remarkably alike: heaps of basalt or crumbling tuffs that weather into deep, rich black soil. Although much eroded, the islands north of Montserrat exhibit characteristic cone-shaped forms, and all have craters now long extinct. St. Christopher is a chain of jagged craters culminating in Mt. Misery (4330 feet). Nevis and the Dutch islands of Saba and St. Eustatius are essentially single cones. The cone on Nevis rises symmetrically to 3596 feet and is so precipitous that all cultivation must be done with the spade, except on the narrow coastal plain. Montserrat, on the other hand, does not have the characteristic cone shape but is a rugged, deeply ravined, and heavily wooded mass of old volcanic rock (maximum elevation about 3000 feet), with only sulphur vents and small extinct craters as evidence of its former volcanic activity.

Of the outer calcareous islands, Anguilla and Barbuda are low and flat. While the rocks of Barbuda are composed entirely of shell, a large part of Anguilla is strewn with coral heads and boulders. Most of Barbuda is little more than 5 feet above the sea, but on its east side a terraced table-land rises to 205 feet. There are no streams or springs on either island; the soil of both is thin; and both have a cover of low scrub, although Barbuda supports a few good-sized trees.

Like Guadeloupe (see p. 59), Antigua, the largest island of the British Leeward Islands Colony, belongs partly to the calcareous and partly to the volcanic group. A dissected limestone plateau 100 to 200 feet high in

TABLE I—LEEWARD ISLANDS OF GREAT BRITAIN: CLIMATIC DATA.

Station	Temperature (degrees F.)			Rainfall (inches)
	Mean (Annual)	Mean (Warmest month)	Mean (Coolest month)	Mean (Annual)
St. John's (Antigua)	79.5	82.0 (Aug.)	76.9 (Jan.)	49.38
Basseterre (St. Christopher)	78.9	81.4 (Aug.)	76.2 (Feb.)	49.73
Plymouth (Montserrat)	80.0	82.0 (Aug.)	76.0 (Jan.)	68.99

the northeast is separated by a central plain from a small, rugged, wooded massif of volcanic tuffs rising to 1330 feet in the southwest. The result is a variety of soils not found on any of the other islands of the Leeward Islands Colony—fertile volcanic soils in the southwest, heavy clayey soils on the plain, and highly calcareous soils in the northeast.

CLIMATE

The climate of all the islands of the British Leeward Islands Colony is delightful from the end of November to the beginning of May, when the trade winds begin to fail and the hot season sets in. Detailed climatic data are available only for St. John's, Basseterre, and Plymouth.[4] Nevis may be assumed to have much the same climate as the near-by islands of St. Christopher and Montserrat. Anguilla is reported as having an annual temperature range between 75° F. and 85° F. All of the islands are subject to frequent droughts, and the rainfall in Anguilla is particularly irregular. On the Virgin Islands the average rainfall is about 55 inches, and the temperature range is about the same as on Antigua, with the temperature rarely rising above 90° F. and often falling below 65° F. All the islands are in the path of the West Indian hurricanes, but really disastrous occurrences are not frequent.

[4]*Monthly Weather Review*, Vol. 54, 1926, pp. 150–151.

Historical Note

The Leeward Islands were discovered by Columbus on his second voyage in 1493, but no settlements were made by the Spanish. The first island to be colonized was St. Christopher, where a small company of Englishmen was landed in 1623. In 1627 a French party, commissioned by Richelieu, landed on the island after a disastrous voyage on which more than half the party died on shipboard. They were received by the Englishmen with great kindness, and the island was amicably divided with them, the Englishmen taking the middle part and the Frenchmen the two ends. British colonists from St. Christopher established settlements on

TABLE II—LEEWARD ISLANDS OF GREAT BRITAIN: AREAS AND
ESTIMATED POPULATION, 1938

Island and Chief Town	Population	Area (sq. mi.)	Density (per sq. mi.)	Composition (per cent)			Birth Rate (per 1000)	Death Rate (per 1000)
				White	Mixed	Negro		
Antigua St. John's	34,123 10,000	108	316	4.0	13.0	83.0	41.50	22.50
St. Christopher Basseterre	17,886 8,000	68	263	4.6	16.3	79.1	45.86	31.99
Nevis Charlestown	13,966 1,200	56	264	0.9	12.6	86.5	28.40	11.17
Anguilla	5,717	34	168	2.2	25.2	72.6	26.76	13.12
Montserrat Plymouth	13,670 2,000	32	427	1.0	21.0	78.0	34.20	15.40
Virgin Islands Roadtown	6,364 400	67	95	1.0	23.0	76.0	37.54	24.30

Nevis in 1628 and on Antigua and Montserrat in 1632, for even at this early date the British section of St. Christopher was rapidly becoming overcrowded. Barbuda was colonized from Antigua in 1661. The first settlement in what is now the British Virgin Islands was made by the Dutch in 1648. Tortola in the Virgin Islands was taken from the Dutch in 1672, and in 1680 its settlement by colonists from Anguilla began.

In 1640 the Carib Indians completely devastated Antigua and, though driven off, continued their raids on various islands until as late as 1796. British possession of the islands was also frequently contested by the French during the wars of the seventeenth and eighteenth centuries but since 1793 has been unchallenged. The present islands of the colony, with Dominica, were brought under a single government in 1832. Dominica, however, was transferred to the Windward Islands Colony in 1940.

POPULATION

No census of the Leeward Islands Colony has been taken since 1921. The estimates given in Table II are based on the rate of increase between the census of 1911 and this last census. Barbuda, for which detailed estimates are not available, has a population of about 1000, practically all of whom are of mixed or pure Negro blood.

TRANSPORTATION AND COMMUNICATIONS

In normal times steamships of the Canadian National Line call fortnightly at Antigua, St. Christopher, and Montserrat on their way to and from Barbados, Trinidad, and British Guiana. A British line and two United States lines, running from New York to Barbados, Trinidad, and ports beyond, call about once every two weeks. As there is no direct line from Great Britain, connection is made by way of Barbados, New York, or Canadian ports. French and Dutch steamships en route to their own near-by colonies also call at St. Christopher and Antigua. Pan American Airways planes flying between Miami and Georgetown and Paramaribo (Dutch Guiana) make weekly stops in each direction at Antigua.

The colony has telegraphic connection with the outside world by cable, with stations on Antigua and St. Christopher, and by radiotelegraph, with stations on Antigua, St. Christopher, and Montserrat, which communicate with each other and with the station at Barbados for outside communications. A coast station is also maintained on St. Christopher for communication with ships at sea. There are government-operated telephone systems on Antigua, St. Christopher, Nevis, and Montserrat.

ECONOMIC AND SOCIAL CONDITIONS ON THE INDIVIDUAL ISLANDS

Antigua. Sugar is by far the most important product of Antigua. The export value in 1938 was £194,470, while the other exports totaled only £25,551, £12,676 of which was accounted for by molasses and rum, also cane products. Antigua's two sugar factories are independent of the plantations—a highly efficient one at Gunthorpes with a capacity of about 25,000 tons and a much less efficient one at Bendals with a capacity of about 4000 tons. Although the greater part of the cane comes from the large estates, cane is also raised by the small proprietors and sold to the factories in sufficient quantities to justify recent extensions of the light railway system that feeds the factories. Sea-island cotton is now the second most important product of Antigua, with about 1300 acres in the crop in 1938 and an export value of £11,910.

On Antigua a much larger proportion of the land is not suitable for cane though suitable for growing food crops than is the case on other predominantly sugar islands such as St. Christopher and Barbados. Although it is reported that there are some hundreds of small holdings on land of this type, the total area contained in them must be small, since the various royal commissions that have studied the island's economic and social problems in recent years have all recommended large-scale governmental settlement schemes as their solution. A large number of laborers on the sugar estates rent small plots, and there is also a practice on a number of the estates of assigning their laborers free plots for growing food crops.

The result is that a large part of the food of the laboring class is grown locally. Also, a good deal of livestock is raised for local consumption, and fish, locally caught, plays an important part in the diet. Import duties on food are high, but this should probably be considered a double blessing, since it not only promotes local cultivation of food crops but checks the consumption of polished rice and white flour. Housing is good as compared with most of the housing of the laboring class elsewhere in the Caribbean area. Most of even the agricultural laborers live in their own houses in villages and in St. John's. The characteristic dwellings provided for laborers on the estates are substantial stone houses, although too frequently they have only one room. A government-subsidized housing scheme is making progress and proving a general incentive for the building of new and better houses.

The agricultural estates are the chief market for labor. Wages and the standard of living are low, and, while there is little actual unemployment, much of the employment is on a part-time or seasonal basis. The disadvantage of part-time and seasonal work is to some extent offset by the arrangements permitting workers to cultivate near-by land for food crops in their spare time. Formerly there was a market for labor in the United States, Puerto Rico, Cuba, and the Dominican Republic, but the United States and Puerto Rican market is now closed, and the decline of the sugar market has ended the need for extra labor on the Cuban sugar plantations. There still is, however, a limited demand for seasonal labor on the Dominican sugar plantations. A land-settlement scheme with the object of relieving the labor situation by increasing the number of self-sustaining peasant proprietors is being actively pushed and shows much promise.

Barbuda, a dependency of Antigua, with an area of 62 square miles (nearly the size of St. Christopher), was never fully colonized. In the possession of the Codrington family from 1691 to 1872, it was used by them as a stock farm for their Antiguan estates and as a shooting preserve. It has a population of about 900, almost exclusively mixed bloods and Negroes engaged chiefly in subsistence farming. A government stock farm on the island offers some employment.

St. Christopher-Nevis. The sugar exported from the presidency in 1938 (valued at £203,984) and the molasses (valued at £12,044) came principally from cane grown on St. Christopher, although some cane is also grown on Nevis and sold to the St. Christopher factory and some muscovado sugar and fancy molasses are made there in old-fashioned mills. Nevis once had a number of flourishing sugar estates and a larger population than at present, but a number of developments, culminating in the erection of the presidency's only modern factory on St. Christopher, ruined the industry. On the other hand, practically all of the sea-island cotton exported from the presidency in 1938 (£4193) came from Nevis, where its production is steadily increasing, the value of the 1938 crop exceeding that of 1937 by £15,605. Some sea-island cotton is also grown on Anguilla, a dependency of St. Christopher-Nevis, but that island's chief product is salt evaporated from sea water, £3240 worth of which was exported in 1938.

The population of Nevis consists of some 600 proprietors of holdings of about an acre, or at most of a few acres, each and of a very much larger number of share croppers engaged in growing chiefly food crops but also some cane and sea-island cotton. Since the ruin of the sugar industry on the island the estate owners, many of them absentee, have developed the system of share cropping in the hope of getting an income from their land. The population of Anguilla is made up almost exclusively of small proprietors. On St. Christopher, owing to the high value of the cultivable land for export products, there are few small holdings, and the population consists chiefly of agricultural laborers, about 7000 persons being engaged in sugar cultivation. The island's one sugar factory, a modern, highly efficient plant, employs 400 to 600 more, and government work, harbor work, etc. account for about 2500. Some labor is also drawn from Nevis and Anguilla during the peak season in the sugar industry. There is no really serious unemployment on any of the islands, although a good deal of the work available to the townspeople is part time or seasonal only.

Although rather more provision is made on the St. Christopher estates than on any of the other islands of the colony for housing agricultural labor, housing conditions both on the estates and in the villages are bad, with very few sanitary facilities. Basseterre, the principal town, has bad slums.

Wages are low, the average for unskilled labor being 1s. 2d. (28 cents) a day. The cost of living, however, is also low, running about 5s. to 7s. ($1.20 to $1.68) a week, and a good deal of wild or semiwild food (breadfruit, mangoes, etc.) is to be had for the picking. On the estates the laborers are generally allotted land for growing vegetables, and in the hills there is much rough land available to the laborers for pasturing livestock, since the sugar plantations are confined to the relatively flat lands bordering the island.

Montserrat. Sea-island cotton is the chief product of Montserrat, although the export value of the crop in 1938, owing to unfavorable weather conditions and the consequent development of pests and disease, was only £26,630 as compared with £44,860 in 1937. Tomato cultivation by the small proprietors is developing; the export in 1938, which went mostly to Canada, was valued at £5568. Lime products (raw lime juice, fresh fruit, and lime oil) are now third among the exports, with a total value of £2800 in 1938, but the market for these is not large enough to promise any important development of the industry.

The population of Montserrat is made up largely of small proprietors and share croppers, with a preponderance of the latter. Since both classes are to a great extent engaged in raising food crops, there is no really serious unemployment problem. Housing seems fairly satisfactory, and many new houses, to some extent of reinforced concrete, have been built during the past few years to replace buildings destroyed by earthquakes. The work on the estates, where the main crop is cotton, is done on a share system, with funds advanced to the workers against their crop. Recently there has been some hardship because of poor cotton crops, but no lack of food, which is locally grown on a large scale, the surplus going to St. Christopher.

Virgin Islands. The principal export product of the Virgin Islands is beef cattle, which find a market in the neighboring Virgin Islands of the United States. Cotton is the principal cultivated crop, and, although it has suffered badly of late from the boll weevil, experts strongly recommend its development. A five-year plan has been devised and put into operation to establish the industry, and a grant of £500 to fight pests was reported in 1938.

With the majority of the inhabitants small proprietors and fishermen, there is no unemployment problem of importance. In fact, the wage-earning population is small and almost entirely limited to Roadtown on Tortola Island. Housing on the Virgin Islands is better than on the other islands of the Leeward Islands Colony; the usual peasant house is of fair size, is sturdily built, and stands on an acre or more of ground. Of the other inhabited islands, Anegada has a population of about 360 engaged in fishing and salvaging, and Virgin Gorda possibly a score more engaged in raising stock and vegetables and burning charcoal for the St. Thomas market.

WINDWARD ISLANDS OF GREAT BRITAIN

Government. The Windward Islands Colony of Great Britain, consisting of the administrative units of Dominica, St. Lucia, St. Vincent, and Grenada, is not a federated colony like the Leeward Islands Colony and has no common legislative body, laws, or tariffs. There are, however, a Governor and a Colonial Secretary in common, whose seat is at St. George's on Grenada. Dominica, St. Lucia, and St. Vincent each have an Administrator and an Executive Council appointed by the crown, while the Colonial Secretary acts as Administrator of Grenada when the Governor is absent. Each island has a Legislative Council of official and nonofficial members appointed by the crown and a minority of members elected under limited franchise. Dominica formerly belonged to the Leeward Islands Colony but was attached to the Windward Islands group on January 1, 1940. The Grenadines are divided administratively between St. Vincent and Grenada.

PHYSICAL FEATURES

The islands of the Windward Islands Colony trend in a generally southward direction from the French island of Guadeloupe. Martinique, also French, separates Dominica, the northernmost island of the colony, from the others.

Like the inner chain of the Leeward Islands Colony the islands of the Windward Islands Colony are all of volcanic origin, but, as on Montserrat and the Basse Terre section of Guadeloupe, erosion has destroyed the symmetry of most of the cones. The characteristic land forms are deeply ravined piles of weathered basalt and volcanic tuffs with many old craters, and there is evidence of volcanic activity in sulphur vents (*soufrières*) and hot springs.

Dominica (305 sq. mi.) is the largest British island in the Lesser Antilles and in Morne Diablotin (5204 ft.) rises to the highest elevation in the whole chain. Boiling Lake, a sulphur geyser in the southern part, still shows intermittent activity, and there was an eruption of fine ash in this region in 1880. So rugged is the central mountain mass that no road crosses the island.

St. Lucia, St. Vincent, the Grenadines, and Grenada form an unbroken line of British possessions south of Martinique. Over the greater part of St. Lucia (223 sq. mi.) the volcanic materials have been eroded into mature forms with broad open valleys and show no trace of the original cones. In the center of the western slope of the main north-south range, however, a number of younger volcanic forms still retain their conical shapes. A considerable area at the southwest end of the island is covered by a mud flow that slopes gently to the sea. The highest point on the island, Morne Gimie, rises to 3145 feet. Gros Piton (2619 feet) and Petit Piton (2481 feet), two remarkably steep, sharp-pointed peaks rising sheer from the sea on the west coast, are believed to be volcanic plugs.

At the northern end of St. Vincent (150 sq. mi.) the enormous cone of Soufrière rises to 4048 feet. After lying dormant for 90 years (there was a disastrous eruption in 1812), this volcano erupted in 1902, synchronously with the eruption of Mt. Pelée in Martinique, devastating the whole northern part of the island and killing some 2000 people. The southern half of St. Vincent is in an advanced stage of dissection, although more youthful in form than St. Lucia. Here, from a main north-south axial range numerous rough spurs run down to the sea. On the west side of the range these spurs are steep and sharp-crested, with deep, narrow gorges between them; but on the east they are more gently sloping, and the valleys are wider and flatter and in a number of cases open into fairly extensive coastal plains.

The Grenadines form a chain of about 100 small islands and rocks extending for a distance of 60 miles between St. Vincent and Grenada. The

TABLE III—WINDWARD ISLANDS OF GREAT BRITAIN: CLIMATIC DATA.

	Temperature (degrees F.)			Rainfall (inches)	
	Mean (Annual)	Mean (Warmest Month)	Mean (Coolest month)	Mean (Annual)	1938
Roseau (Dominica)	80.0	82.2 (Sept.)	77.2 (Feb.)	77.64	104.6
Port Castries (St. Lucia)	78.6	80.6 (Sept.)	75.6 (Jan.)	91.0	128.9
Kingstown (St. Vincent)	79.2	81.0 (Sept.)	77.0 (Jan.)	90.8	104.49
St. George's (Grenada)	78.9	80.4 (Sept.)	77.1 (Jan.)	76.56	116.38

two largest are Carriacou (about 13 sq. mi.), near the southern end of the chain, and Bequia (about 9 sq. mi.), at the northern end. All of them are very much worn-down volcanic residuals (the highest elevations are Union Island, near the center of the chain, 1010 feet; Carriacou, 980; Bequia, 880).

Grenada (133 sq. mi.) consists of a main north-south axial range of maturely dissected volcanic rocks extended westward at its southern end by a series of subdued volcanic hills. The island has the appearance of being tilted down from northwest to southeast, with steep slopes much cliffed and little embayed on the northwest side and long, gentle, deeply embayed slopes on the southeast. Most of the embayments on both sides are partially delta-filled. The island is the lowest in the Windward Islands group (highest elevation 2749 feet). At present there seems to be no evidence of volcanic activity.

CLIMATE

The figures (Table III) show that temperature and rainfall conditions are much the same in the several islands of the Windward Islands Colony.

It is to be noted that these figures on temperature and rainfall are for only one place on each island and that on the west side. It is to be assumed that temperatures are in general a few degrees lower, and the rainfall somewhat higher, on the east side, which is exposed to the trade winds, than on the sheltered west side. Rainfall records at various points on all the islands show, however, that the greatest variation in the amount of rainfall is produced by differences in elevation. On Dominica, for example, the annual mean increases from 77.64 inches at Roseau to 105 inches at St. Aroment (elevation 360 feet), only two miles to the northeast, and to 185 inches at Shawford (elevation 500 feet) a mile farther in the same direction. The rainfall on all the islands was exceptionally heavy in 1938.

TABLE IV—WINDWARD ISLANDS OF GREAT BRITAIN: AREAS AND
ESTIMATED POPULATION, 1938

Island and Chief Town	Popu- lation	Area (sq. mi.)	Density (per sq. mi.)	Composition (per cent)				Birth rate (per 1000)	Death rate (per 1000)
				White	Mixed	Negro	East Indian		
Dominica Roseau	50,617 8,000	305	166	1.5	31.5	67.0	....	29.52	19.98
St. Lucia Castries	69,084 21,000	233	309	....	....	....	....	30.70	14.80
St. Vincent Kings- town	58,381 4,000	150	389	2.5	23.5	69.5	4.5	37.94	17.80
Grenada St. George's	88,201 5,000	133	665	1.5	17.5	77.0	4.0	29.80	15.20

All the islands have numerous streams, most of which carry water even during the driest months, and such descriptions as are available indicate that, outside the cultivated sections, all are heavily forested.

HISTORICAL NOTE

The islands were discovered by Columbus, but no attempt at colonization was made by the Spanish or others for more than a hundred years after their discovery. The first important settlements were made by the French on Grenada in 1625, on Dominica in 1635, and on St. Lucia in 1650, and by the British on St. Vincent in 1762. From their earliest settlement to 1804, when they passed permanently into British control, the history of these islands is one of almost constant shifting between French and British sovereignty. Dominica changed hands no less than fifteen times. Evidence of French occupation of all the islands is to be found in the many French names not only of physical features but of towns and villages, and a French patois is still the prevailing language of the mass of the people on Dominica and St. Lucia, and to a considerable extent on Grenada.

The organization of the islands for administrative purposes has also gone through many changes. In 1833 St. Vincent, Grenada, Barbados, and Tobago were brought together under one general government—the Windward Islands Colony; and Dominica was assigned to the Leeward Islands Colony. In 1838 St. Lucia was included in the Windward Islands Colony. Barbados was separated from it in 1885 and Tobago attached to Trinidad in 1889. Finally Dominica was included in 1940.

POPULATION

No census has been taken of any of the islands of the Windward Islands Colony since 1921, and the estimates in Table IV are based on the rate of increase between the 1911 census and this date. Estimates on the racial composition of the population of St. Lucia could not be obtained, but it probably does not differ greatly from that of the population of Dominica. There are very few East Indians on either of these islands.

TRANSPORTATION AND COMMUNICATIONS

In normal times all the islands of the Windward Islands Colony have direct fortnightly passenger, mail, and freight service by the Canadian National Line to and from Canada, the United States, Bermuda, the other British West Indies (except Jamaica), and British Guiana. Similar service is afforded by United States passenger and freight lines, and there is also a fortnightly freight service to and from Canada. Frequent but irregular connection with Great Britain is made by British steamers on their way to and from Barbados, Trinidad, and British Guiana, as well as by transfer to the regular transatlantic services at Barbados, New York, or Canadian ports. None of the islands are regular stops on the Pan American Airways West Indian route between Miami and Georgetown and Paramaribo, the nearest connections being the regular stops on the French islands of Martinique and Guadeloupe or on Antigua in the Leeward Islands Colony. French steamers en route to the near-by French colonies also make frequent stops.

All the islands have cable connection with the outside world through the Cable and Wireless (West Indies) Ltd. system. This company also has a radio and telegraph station on Dominica and one at St. George's, Grenada, but the latter is not normally in operation. There is a coast station for radiotelegraph on St. Lucia for communication with ships at sea, and a government-owned station on Carriacou connects Grenada with Barbados.

Transportation connections between the islands are by the regular steamships of the West Indian lines and by local sailing vessels and tramp steamers. There are no railroads, but all the islands except Dominica have fairly good road systems.

On Dominica, because of the mountainous relief, the many rivers, and the menace of frequent landslides, roads are very difficult to construct and maintain; only about 68 miles of road are at all suitable for motor traffic, and only a few miles, in the vicinity of Roseau, are first class. Launch service is generally used between Roseau and Portsmouth, the two main towns (about 20 miles apart), most of the "road" between them being a bridle path. St. Lucia is well served with 62.5 miles of main roads, 88 miles of second-class roads (also suitable for motor traffic), and some 230 miles of unclassified roads. St. Vincent has about 26 miles of oiled roads, about 41 miles of macadam, and 330 miles of dirt roads and bridle paths. Grenada is particularly fortunate in having a first-class bitumen-surfaced road running completely around the island, as well as a large mileage of surface-treated second-class roads suitable for motor traffic. All the towns are connected by motorbus service. None of the islands have telegraph systems, but all have fairly adequate telephone service, Grenada being by far the best equipped, with 6500 miles of trunk and subscribers' lines and 516 subscribers in 1936.

HARBORS

None of the islands of the Windward Islands Colony have harbors or even sheltered anchorages suitable for large ships on their east sides, but all of them have a number of good roadsteads on their west sides, and there are several harbors capable of accommodating a considerable number of ships of deep draft. Of these the best are Port Castries on St. Lucia (one of the most secure harbors in the West Indies), Kingstown Bay on St. Vincent (an indentation 1500 yards long and 1¼ miles wide with depths of 18 to 20 fathoms over practically the whole area), and St. George's Bay on Grenada (with a small inner basin suitable for deep-draft ships and a well sheltered roadstead). All of these are equipped with wharves (with low-water level alongside of 18 to 20 feet at Kingstown and St. George's and 29 to 30 feet at Port Castries) and have radio stations and good supplies of fresh water. The many islands of the Grenadines afford a large number of fairly good roadsteads capable of accommodating in the aggregate a large number of ships, while Admiralty Bay on Bequia Island, Charlestown Bay on Cannouan Island, and Tyrell Bay on Carriacou are well sheltered anchorages, although without service facilities of any sort.

ECONOMIC AND SOCIAL CONDITIONS ON THE INDIVIDUAL ISLANDS

Dominica. Dominica, never an important sugar island, now produces no sugar. Coffee, important in colonial times, is now no longer produced, although there is much land suitable for it. Lime products (fresh limes, raw and concentrated juice, and lime oil) are the leading exports, with a total value in 1938 of £22,212, of which nearly half was that of distilled oil. The other exports (mostly tree products) in the order of their importance were: bananas (£8115), coconuts and copra (£5400), oranges (£5330), bay oil (£3936), vanilla (£3755), cacao (£3292), mangoes (£2306), grapefruit (£1894), avocados (£1320), tobacco (£1259), rum (£697), hardwood (£211). Lime trees were almost wiped out a few years ago by a root disease, but they have been replaced with trees grafted on resistant stock, and the production is rapidly increasing; the total crop in 1938 was nearly 59,000 barrels, compared with 27,000 in 1934. The fresh-fruit trade, especially in grapefruit, is steadily expanding, and the coconut industry shows considerable revival as the result of recent improvement in the copra market and coöperative operations by the growers. A large proportion of all export crops is produced by the small proprietors, who make up the greater part of the population. There is still much undeveloped land suited to various tree crops.

Since there is practically no coastal plain on Dominica, there is little land on which sugar could be grown. This partly explains why Dominica is the most thinly populated of all the West Indian islands. The population is very largely made up of small proprietors. The only markets for the labor of the wage earners on the island, estimated at about 1000 in number, are stevedoring and work on the estates, which demand no such amount of labor as do the sugar plantations elsewhere. Most of the estates are owned by local planters, only a few by absentee European owners. Unemployment is not a really serious problem, since the number of wage earners is small, their standards of living low, and food cheap even for the few who do not have opportunities to raise it. However, not only among the laboring class but among the small proprietors as well, ready money is generally lacking for the necessities of life that the island does not produce.

Dominica is in general considered healthful, although the death rate in 1938 was the highest in the Windward Islands Colony, and infant mortality is high. The food supply is good, consisting largely of locally grown vegetables and fish. Livestock is raised, although not enough to provide sufficient meat and milk for the poorer classes. The housing standard is somewhat higher than that on the neighboring islands; most of the dwellings are divided into more than one room, but, as elsewhere in the islands, there are usually no arrangements for sanitation. In Roseau and Portsmouth, the two towns, many houses have been built by landlords and are rented for 3s. to 4s. 6d. (72 cents to $1.08) a week. A large proportion of the country dwellers, on the other hand, live in houses on their own land built by themselves from local lumber.

St. Lucia. Sugar is the chief product of St. Lucia, although of about 22,000 acres under cultivation only about 4300 are in cane. Its cultivation is principally confined to four large plantations, each of which has its own factory. A small proportion of the cane is cultivated under a share-crop system, and some fairly large areas are grown by small proprietors. About 750 tons of sugar are retained for local use and the remainder is exported to Great Britain and Canada. Exports of sugar in 1938 were valued at £64,711. The other principal exports in the order of their value were: lime products £14,429, bananas £13,568, coconuts and copra £11,184, cacao £8332, molasses £3086, mangoes £1900. The lime and coconut industries are almost exclusively confined to the large estates. The lime industry has suffered rather badly of late from pests and root disease: the 1938 crop, 28,294 barrels as compared with 34,048 in 1937, was the poorest since 1932. Unfavorable weather and poor prices for cacao in 1938 have further diminished interest in this once important crop.

Although there are very few small landowners on St. Lucia, the share-crop system has had considerable development of late. Until recently no attempt has been made at land settlement with a view to increasing the number of small proprietors, in spite of the fact that there is a good deal of cultivable land not under cultivation which could be used for the purpose. In 1939, however, a land-settlement project involving some 2000 acres was reported as about to be undertaken. The Barbados government is carrying out a similar scheme at the southern end of St. Lucia, where selected Barbadian agriculturists will be brought in (see p. 33).

As on all the islands where the proportion of small proprietors is small, the food of the laboring class tends to be largely farinaceous, although fresh and salted fish, locally caught, are widely consumed, and, as in most of the islands of the Lesser Antilles, wild and semiwild fruit may be had for the picking. Housing is in general of very low standard, although on the estates that provide dwellings for their laborers many old houses have recently been replaced by concrete buildings with baths and sanitation. Castries, the chief town, has some bad slum areas, but they are small.

The estates are the chief market for labor, with the usual part-time and seasonal work afforded by the handling and shipping of the agricultural products. The sugar estates employ about 6000 laborers, but about half of these are engaged only while the crop is in process of cultivation and harvesting. Lime cultivation and the extracting industry connected with it ordinarily employ about 1000 fairly constantly, but with the present poor prices, production is being decreased and the employment of labor consequently declining. The coconut industry employs about 1400 throughout the year, bananas account for about 1000 more, cacao 600, and coaling at Castries 500 (although coaling is declining, this station is still of some importance). The labor supply, however, is believed to be about 30 to 40 per cent above the normal demand, and in 1939 the Labor Commissioner of the island estimated that work was needed for about 8000, although the problem was considered one of part-time work rather than complete lack of work. The depression has affected particularly the lime and cacao plantations, where there seems to be little chance of recovery.

St. Vincent. The leading exports of St. Vincent in the order of their importance in 1938 were: arrowroot (£91,638), sea-island cotton (£60,260), coconuts and copra (£12,739), syrup and molasses (£12,317), bananas (£2759), sugar (£2003), rum (about £1500), Marie Galante cotton (£1094), cacao (£751). Not only is arrowroot the chief product, but St. Vincent has practically a world monopoly of this crop. Small proprietors grow considerably more than a fourth of the arrowroot and more than half of the sea-island cotton; the Marie Galante cotton (grown in the Grenadines) is produced under a share-crop system. Practically all the cane is grown on the estates. The island has only one small sugar factory, and it is of interest that syrup rather than sugar is the principal cane product. Coconuts, of which the estimated average production is 5300 each year, are also all grown on the estates and are of very high quality. The bananas are all shipped to Canada. Their cultivation was formerly confined mostly to the estates but is now tending to shift to the small holdings, as losses from wind and disease have discouraged the maintenance of large acreages. A good deal of rum is distilled, largely for local consumption (in 1938 26,858 gallons out of a total output of 40,345 gallons were locally consumed).

Although the greater part of the island is still in large estates, there is a large number of small proprietors. In 1937 11,352 acres were in lots of less than 10 acres and 4924 acres in lots of 11 to 50 acres. Plantations, some of them of 1000 acres or more, totaled 37,556 acres, but a number of these include considerable uncultivable land.

Although flour, rice, and salt fish are imported (the total expenditure for these items in 1937 was £36,691 or considerably less than £1 per person), they play a really small part in the average diet, which must at best be scanty when it is considered that so much of the employment on the island is intermittent. More locally grown meat is consumed than in most of the neighboring islands, but it still contributes too little to the diet. Wild and semiwild products, breadfruit, mangoes, etc., however, are fairly abundant, and fish caught locally is an important element in the diet. Housing is in general very poor. The owners of the estates have made little provision for houses for laborers, although where this has been done the houses are good. The building of houses by the laborers themselves on estate land is common and the results are usually small and very poorly constructed, and the standard of houses built by the small proprietors is also low. Even in Kingstown, small as it is in population, there is much overcrowding and poor building.

In 1938 it was estimated that 14,507 persons were engaged in agricultural labor, 4267 in various trades, and 3016 in domestic service. Most of the work on the estates is seasonal, however, so that while there may be little total unemployment, a very high proportion of the laboring population has to live on part-time earnings, supplemented by what vegetables they may have opportunity to raise, what fish they may catch, and what wild food they may be able to gather. In 1937 there were about 1000 persons on charity, and some 400 more were receiving aid from poor-relief funds. There is some recruiting of labor, under written contract, for work in connection with oil refining on Aruba in the Netherlands West Indies.

Although the St. Vincent government has followed for some time a policy of acquiring land for subdivision into small holdings, it has been seriously handicapped by the fact that not only is good land rarely for sale but the price is too high for any large-scale settlement scheme.

Grenada. Cacao is the chief product of Grenada (export value in 1935 £126,920), with nutmegs (export value in 1938 £74,625) second in importance. The other leading export products in 1938 were: mace (£38,995), bananas (£11,134), lime oil (£9735), cotton (£2588), cotton seed (£1276). In spite of the predominance of small proprietors, most of the export products are grown on the large estates owing to the practice by the small proprietors of serving as laborers on the estates and using their own land chiefly for growing food. The cotton export, which comes from Carriacou, in the Grenada section of the Grenadines, is grown by small proprietors, who also produce considerable quantities of fruits and vegetables for sale on the neighboring islands.

The number of small proprietors on Grenada is unusually large. In 1938 there were 18,004 holdings of less than 10 acres, totaling 24,977 acres; 352 of 11 to 50, totaling 7187; 58 of 51 to 100, totaling 4257; and 130 of 101 to 1000 acres, totaling 37,575 acres. Government settlement began on Carriacou in 1903 and on Grenada in 1909, and there are now 19 settlement projects on the two, totaling 3868 acres. The effect of this large percentage of small proprietors is said to be reflected in the generally intelligent, clean, and energetic appearance of the people.

Although there is the usual overweighting of the diet with farinaceous food, there appears to be no real lack of food. On the estates it is a rather general practice to give the employees land for gardens, and there is usually an opportunity to obtain rough land for pasturing. In St. George's, the chief town, housing in general is reported as satisfactory, and the town as a whole is remarkably clean; but in the country the houses are extremely poor, in spite of the fact that there are many small proprietors. The practice of using imported lumber—although there is apparently no lack of local timber—may largely account for the poor houses on an island that seems otherwise the most prosperous in the British islands of the Lesser Antilles. Furthermore, in most cases the houses of the laborers on the estates, though owned by the laborers themselves, are built on land let rent-free or at a low charge, a practice not conducive to good housing. Mud-and-wattle huts with cane-straw roofs are used to some extent by the poorer classes.

Owing to the decline in the market for the island's specialized crops, there is a good deal of part-time employment at present and considerable unemployment.

The Grenadines. In the St. Vincent section of the Grenadines, of which Bequia Island is the most important, cultivation, mainly cotton for export and food crops, is chiefly on a share-crop system carried on by the women, the men being largely engaged in fishing and boat building. Carriacou, the principal island of the Grenada section, is divided into small farm holdings, with only two large plantations remaining. Housing is decidedly above the average in the West Indies, and the inhabitants are prosperous, except for lack of ready money for things that the island does not produce.

BARBADOS

Government. Executive branch: Governor, Executive Council appointed by the crown, and Executive Committee consisting of official members of the Executive Council and one member from the Legislative Council and four from the House of Assembly nominated annually by the Governor. Legislative branch: Governor, Legislative Council of nine members appointed by the crown, and House of Assembly of 24 members elected for a two-year period under a limited franchise.

Physical Features

Barbados Colony consists of a single isolated island (166 sq. mi.) about 102 miles due east of St. Vincent Island of the Windward Islands Colony. Geologically as well, Barbados appears to stand apart from the other islands of the West Indies. It contains no volcanic rock but has a core of strongly folded sandstones and dark sandy clays overlain by deep beds of calcareous and silicious marine deposits, which, in turn, over six-sevenths of the surface are covered with coral limestone. The highest point (1104 feet) is in a range of rounded hills near the center of the island. Coral reefs fringe the east, west, and south shores, in places extending three miles out to sea. The soil, though shallow, is of high fertility and has a considerable element of volcanic material, presumably from Soufrière on St. Vincent, from which during the eruption of 1902—which occurred synchronously with that of Mt. Pelée on Guadeloupe—ashes fell on all parts of the island. Originally Barbados was largely covered with forest, chiefly mahogany, locust, and fustic, but now is almost completely under cultivation. Owing to the porous character of the coralline surface, there are no surface streams of any account, and water is obtained from subterranean channels and wells.

CLIMATE

The climate is healthful. The temperature, tempered during eight months of the year by the northeast trades, is remarkably constant. The mean annual temperature at Bridgetown is 79.6° F., with the mean temperature for the hottest month (August) 81° F. and for the coolest month (February) 77.8° F. The average annual rainfall for the island is about 62½ inches. June to November is the rainy season, with September the rainiest month. The driest months, which are also the cool months, are March, April, and the beginning of May. The island is in the path of the West Indian hurricanes and has suffered disastrously on a number of occasions.

HISTORICAL NOTE

The actual date of discovery is unknown, but Barbados is believed to have been first visited by Portuguese. Not only were the British the first to lay claim to the island (allegedly in 1605), but it is the only territory in the Caribbean area that has been continuously in British possession since it was first claimed by a European power. The first settlement, Holetown on the west coast, was made in 1627 by a party of Englishmen. In 1662 the island was created a colony of the British Crown. From 1833 to 1885 it was included with St. Vincent, Grenada, and Tobago in a general government with a Governor-in-Chief resident at Barbados and a Lieutenant-Governor on each of the other islands. When the Windward Islands Colony was constituted in 1885, Barbados was separated and constituted as a separate colony.

Barbados has a long-standing tradition of local representation in government. The date when the House of Assembly was first convened is not known, but it was in existence in 1639 and is thus the third oldest representative body in the British Commonwealth, the British House of Commons being first and the Bermuda House of Assembly second. However, even though the House of Assembly is completely elective, the colony does not have really responsible government, since its Governor, Executive Council, and Legislative Council are appointed and the crown exercises the right of veto. Moreover, although the colony is considered to have the most liberal franchise of any of the British colonies in the Caribbean area, it had only 6381 names on its electoral rolls in 1938.

POPULATION

The estimated population of Barbados in 1938 was 193,082—1163 to the square mile. Estimates of the racial composition in 1938 are not available, but according to the 1921 census it was: white, 7 per cent; mixed blood, 22 per cent; Negro, 71 per cent. The birth rate in 1938 was 27.3 per 1000 and the death rate 19.38. Bridgetown, the capital, has about 15,000 inhabitants, and Speightstown about 1500. Healthful as far as natural conditions are concerned and practically free of tropical diseases, the island is visited as a health resort by people from British Guiana and the near-by islands.

Social Conditions

There are relatively few small proprietors. Out of a total of 68,000 acres (106 sq. mi.) under cultivation, 52,000 are in estates, and the remaining 16,000 are divided into 74 holdings of 20 to 100 acres, 421 of 5 to 20, 517 of 3 to 5, 3905 of 1 to 3, and 13,962 of less than 1 acre. The acreage in holdings of less than 100 acres may seem large when Barbados is compared with neighboring islands but is small when the total population is considered.

The diet of the laboring class is probably poorer and more badly balanced than in any of the other British West Indian islands. Since nearly all the cultivable land is in sugar cane and the population density is far higher than on any of the other islands, there is little opportunity for the home growing of vegetables and no opportunity for the gathering of the wild and semiwild tree foods that contribute to the food supply on the other islands. In fact, vegetables are said to be confined almost exclusively to onions. With the necessity of depending chiefly on imported foodstuffs and with wages low, the cheaper, farinaceous foods naturally predominate in the diet.

The housing of both the workers on the estates and the small proprietors is poor, not so much from the standpoint of construction, which is fairly good, but from that of overcrowding and sanitary facilities. About 75 per cent of the estate workers live in houses which they own but which are built on rented land. In Bridgetown there is not only serious overcrowding within the houses but also much crowding together of the houses, with a resulting sacrifice of light and air and sanitary facilities. With little or no land available except at high prices, any scheme of land settlement would be difficult of accomplishment on the island itself. However, a tract of about 3800 acres at Vieux Fort, at the south end of St. Lucia Island in the Windward Islands Colony, has been taken over by the Barbados government and will eventually provide some outlet for the island's surplus population. There is a small sugar factory on this property, and the settlement project includes a 1900-acre unit that will be divided into holdings each consisting of 4 acres of arable land, 1 acre of other land, and a house, the holdings to be rented or sold on time.

The labor supply, even when there was considerable emigration abroad, has for many years exceeded the demand in all branches of employment. No labor census has been taken since 1921, but at that time 34,157 were employed in agriculture, principally on the sugar plantations, 23,682 in industry, 13,169 in commerce, and 1122 in public works. It was estimated in 1938 that the agricultural laborers had increased to 37,500 but that only about 18,574 of these were employed at any one time. Hence the unemployment problem is not so much one of total unemployment as of intermittent employment. From April, 1938, to March, 1939, an average of 4000 applied to the Government Employment Agency each month for assistance in obtaining work.

PRODUCTION AND TRADE

Sugar-cane products, the principal exports of Barbados, consist of dark crystal sugar, muscovado sugar, molasses, and rum, the value of these in 1938 being: sugar, £683,099; molasses, £505,977; and rum, £9848. The only other export of any significance is sea-island cotton (£233 in 1938). Of the 32,261 acres of cane harvested in 1930, 7000 acres were harvested by small proprietors, whose chief cash crop is cane, although they are now being encouraged to grow arrowroot, ginger, and vegetables as more profitable crops with the present prices of sugar. All exports showed serious decline in 1938 as compared with 1937, sugar by £238,156 and molasses by £49,112. Only 33 acres of sea-island cotton were harvested in 1938.

Barbados does a considerable re-export business, the total being valued at £135,576 in 1938 and consisting chiefly of clothing, cotton piece goods, bags and sacks, butter and butter substitutes, preserved fish, flour, rice, and edible oils, going to British Guiana and the near-by islands.

TRANSPORTATION AND COMMUNICATIONS

Barbados has been much better served by steamship transportation than any of the other British colonies in the Caribbean area except Trinidad. Before the present war direct passenger and freight connections with Great Britain and the European continent were afforded not only by British lines but also by Dutch, French, and German lines. Bridgetown is a port of call of the United States and Canadian lines serving the other islands of the Lesser Antilles and also of several American lines that run between the United States and British Guiana (including the Aluminum Line, which arrives fortnightly from New Orleans) and do not ordinarily stop in the Windward and Leeward Islands. The Pan American Airways West Indian route from Miami to Georgetown and Paramaribo does not touch Barbados. Transportation between the island and Trinidad is afforded, however, by planes of the Royal Dutch Airlines, which land at the government-controlled landing field at Seawell, 7½ miles from Bridgetown.

Telegraphic communication with the outside world is provided by cable and wireless, the principal radiotelegraph station for the Lesser Antilles section of the British Caribbean colonies being at Bridgetown. There is also a local broadcasting station at Bridgetown. A well distributed telephone system has now about 2600 subscribers.

With Barbados so closely cultivated and so densely peopled, road building and maintenance take on a somewhat urban aspect. The island's 166 square miles have 268 miles of main roads and about 270 of secondary roads. The arterial roads running out of Bridgetown have recently been largely resurfaced for heavy motor traffic. Motor buses serve all parts of the island with at least once-a-day schedules for all the country districts.

The only harbor of any importance on Barbados is Carlisle Bay, on the southwest side of the island, on which Bridgetown is located. The outer bay, an indentation about a half mile deep and one and a half miles wide, affords well sheltered anchorage for ships of all types. Only vessels of draft of not more than 14½ feet, however, can dock at the wharves. Larger ships are loaded and unloaded by means of lighters handled by government-owned tugs. Bridgetown is a coal and oil-fueling station and has a small drydock capable of handling vessels of 14-foot draft.

TRINIDAD AND TOBAGO

Government. Executive branch: Governor and Executive Council appointed by the crown. Legislative branch: Governor and Legislative Council (12 official members and 13 nonofficial members—6 appointed and 7 elected under limited franchise from 6 electoral districts on Trinidad and 1 comprising Tobago).

Physical Features

Geologically and physiographically Trinidad and Tobago are outliers of the South American continent. Trinidad (area 1862 sq. mi.) is separated from Venezuela by the Gulf of Paria, which it encloses on the east, and by the narrow entrances to the gulf. The mountain range along the northern edge of the island, with a maximum elevation of 3085 feet, is a continuation of the range that forms the Paria Peninsula of Venezuela. The core of this range consists of crystalline schists with threads of quartz that are in places gold-bearing. Foldings in the sedimentary rocks overlying these old schists are represented both in the main range itself and in two other ranges of hills running roughly parallel to it. The southern and most prominent of these, with elevations up to 600 feet, forms the south rim of the island. The central ridge is so masked by alluvial deposits from the Orinoco as to have little prominence except in one isolated summit (1028 feet). The whole north coast is rocky, and the east coast, beaten by the Atlantic surf, is practically unapproachable.

About 40 per cent of the island is under cultivation, and the remainder consists of forest reserves and undeveloped or waste country. Most of the undeveloped country is in the northern range, in the southern range of hills where development has been initiated only recently and there are no large estates, and in a large district in the southeast corner of the island where topography (there are large areas of swamp and of rough land) and poor soils appear to make forestation the only feasible development.

The sugar plantations form an irregular band averaging 4 or 5 miles in width along the west coast from Port of Spain to a few miles south of San Fernando. Here also is the greatest concentration of the population. The cacao plantations cover a much larger area. They include a strip immediately east of the belt of sugar plantations and of about the same width and, connecting with it, two broad areas north and south of the central range of hills, the northern of which reaches through to the east coast. Other principal areas of cacao plantations are the valleys of the south slope of the western half of the northern range and the southwest peninsula. Coconuts are grown in a narrow strip along the greater part of the east coast, on both coasts of the southwest peninsula, and in numerous scattered plantations throughout the sugar belt.

Although Trinidad has been best known for many years on account of her famous asphalt lake (area 114 acres) at La Brea on the north side of the southwest peninsula, the prosperity of the island today is due chiefly to the petroleum industry, of which the present producing fields are principally located in the same peninsula south of La Brea.

Tobago (116 sq. mi.) lies about 22 miles northeast of Trinidad and consists mainly of a single mountain mass of volcanic origin. Only about one-seventh of the island is under cultivation, the remainder being heavily forested.

CLIMATE

In the latitude of Trinidad the trade winds blow from the east. During the dry season (January to the middle of May) they cross the island without appreciable diminution of force, but during the rest of the year they penetrate only a few miles beyond the east coast. The mean annual temperature at Port of Spain is 77.6° F., with the mean temperature for the hottest month (May) 79° F. and for the coolest month (January) 75.8° F. There are two rainfall maxima, one in July and August, and the other in November. The mean annual rainfall along the west coast is about 60 inches, but on the north coast and in the hills bordering the south coast it rises to 85 inches, and on the east coast to 112. On Tobago the rainy season is from June to December with a relatively dry period in September, the average annual fall being 66 inches. At Scarborough on Tobago the mean annual temperature is 81.12° F., with the mean temperature of the hottest month (September) 84.99° F. and of the coolest month (February) 77° F.

HISTORICAL NOTE

Trinidad and Tobago were discovered by Columbus on his third voyage, in 1498.

Of all the present British islands in the Lesser Antilles, Trinidad is the only one on which Spain made any attempt to follow discovery with settlement. The first Spanish governor was appointed in 1532, which year may be taken as the date of the first attempt at colonization, and the island remained, nominally at least, in Spanish possession until taken by the British in 1797. There was considerable cultivation of cacao in the late seventeenth and early eighteenth centuries but little real progress until 1783, when the king of Spain issued a proclamation opening the island to settlement by Roman Catholic colonists of all nations. The rapid colonization following this proclamation was augmented by the arrival of large numbers of French families driven out of the French islands, particularly Santo Domingo, by the French Revolution. Trinidad was finally assigned to Great Britain by the Treaty of Amiens of 1802 between Great Britain, France, Spain, and Holland.

The early settlers of Tobago were mainly Dutch, the first colony having been founded by Zealanders in 1632. By the Treaty of Aix-la-Chapelle of 1748 the island was declared neutral and open to settlement by all the European powers, but actually possession shifted more or less constantly among Great Britain, France, and Holland, from 1662, when the Dutch company that sponsored the first settlement relinquished its claim to the island, until the Treaty of Paris of 1764 ceded it to Great Britain. This last treaty only served to eliminate Holland from the contest, and it was not until 1814 that Great Britain came into permanent possession.

When the Windward Islands Colony was formed in 1833, Tobago was attached to that colony, of which it remained a part until 1889, when it became an integral part of the Colony of Trinidad. Finally in 1899 it was given the status of a ward in the colony, the name of which was changed to Trinidad and Tobago.

POPULATION

The population of Trinidad according to the 1931 census was 387,425, that of Tobago 25,358. The estimated population of the whole colony in 1937 was 456,000 with estimated densities of 229 to the square mile for Trinidad, and 241 for Tobago. Port of Spain, the capital and chief town, had 70,334 inhabitants in 1931. The other important towns are San Fernando (14,287) and Arima (5072). The birth rate in 1937 was 31.46 per 1000, the death rate 17.36. From the censuses of 1921 and 1931 it is not possible to determine the number of whites, Negroes, and persons of mixed blood. The 1931 census enumerated 137,853 East Indians (about 33 per cent of the total), 5082 Chinese, and 7587 born in the United Kingdom, continental Europe, North America, and South America, who were presumably white. Among the remaining 262,405 not distinguished in the census as white or colored it is to be assumed that the percentage of whites would not be higher than that in Barbados, or 7 per cent.

Not only is the laboring class made up of a mixture of Africans, East Indians, and Chinese, but the white residents also form the most cosmopolitan group in the Caribbean. People of Spanish and French descent predominate—Spanish and French are widely spoken—but the British, Dutch, and Portuguese are also well represented.

SOCIAL CONDITIONS

Both islands have healthful natural conditions, and people of European stock whose forebears have resided there for generations are mentally and physically vigorous. A large part of the housing for laborers on the estates and in the oil fields is furnished by the employers, and on some of the sugar estates and oil fields good progress is being made in housing schemes. Elsewhere the houses are in general very poor. Many of the rural workers live in mud or tapia houses with grass roofs. Both on the estates and in the villages there are survivals of the old barracks type of housing. There is much overbuilding and overcrowding in the towns, particularly in Port of Spain, and the houses in the overbuilt areas are uniformly of poor construction and in bad repair. Of the towns, only Port of Spain has modern water-supply and sewage-disposal systems.

The diet of the laborer in Trinidad is no better than that of the other colonies where the greater part of the population consists of wage earners. There is a considerable number of small holdings, particularly in the hands of the East Indians, who, when the indenture system ended, had a choice of being repatriated or of receiving plots of land. Neither official nor unofficial reports, however, make comment on the contribution to the food supply of produce grown by small proprietors, but it is to be assumed that, as in Barbados, the small proprietors work on the estates and in the oil fields or use their land for export crops and in either case pay little attention to growing food crops. On Tobago the former sugar and cacao plantations have been largely supplanted by small holdings. The proprietors grow much of their own food as well as a good deal for export to Trinidad and work on the few remaining estates only as a means of obtaining cash.

Labor in the principal export-producing industries of Trinidad and Tobago was divided as follows in 1938: sugar plantations and factories, 23,797; cacao, 17,523; petroleum, 14,307; coconuts, 2751; asphalt, 650. The employment in all of these except petroleum and asphalt is largely intermittent.

Trinidad has made much better progress than any of the other British Caribbean colonies in developing manufacturing industries. There are now more than 200 factories producing various products, largely for local consumption, but no figures are available on the amount of labor they employ. Unemployment is not so acute a problem as in most of the other British colonies. In fact there is at times a shortage of labor in certain specialized tasks, and some of the petroleum companies make a practice of recruiting labor from the neighboring islands. Wages are generally somewhat higher than elsewhere in the Lesser Antilles. The really serious problem is the low standard of living resulting from the intermittent character of much of the employment, coupled with rather high costs. Trade unionism is better developed in Trinidad than in any of the other British Caribbean colonies. Strikes developing to riot proportions, with some casualties, broke out in 1937 but were finally settled to the general satisfaction of both sides, collective negotiations on wages and hours having made good progress in most industries.

PRODUCTION AND TRADE

Not only was the value of the petroleum exported from Trinidad ($23,656,561) in 1938 about twice that of all the other exports, but the island now leads all of the British dominions and colonies in petroleum production. Although oil for lamps and for lubricating purposes was refined from asphalt in Trinidad as early as 1856 and actual drilling began in 1867, it was not until 1908 that the first large well was drilled, and the first steamship load of petroleum was not shipped until 1911. Since that time production has steadily increased, and the export value of crude and refined oil and gasoline more than doubled between 1933 and 1938 (exports in 1933, 8,907,298 barrels valued at $10,819,464; in 1938, 16,417,056 barrels valued at $23,656,561). The value of asphalt exports rose from $724,465 in 1933 to $1,194,914 in 1937, with a slight decline in 1938. All the other exports are agricultural, the value of the important ones in 1938 being: sugar, $4,457,963; cacao, $2,369,286; grapefruit, $318,243; coconuts and coconut products, $235,389; limes and lime products, $118,042; angostura bitters, $114,787; rum, $59,314. All of these export figures for 1938 were the lowest since 1935 except those for grapefruit exports, which have been increasing steadily for a number of years. The export value of coconuts and coconut products had been declining for a number of years until 1937 when it rose to $953,134, the highest figure since 1929, but in 1938, owing to a serious slump in the market, it fell to $235,389, the lowest figure in more than a decade. Coffee was once an important product, but there are now very few plantations left. Shipments of bananas, which have only recently begun to be of any importance, were reported as valued at $71,030 in 1936 and $76,930 in 1937, figures for subsequent years not being available. With 860 square miles of forest land still on Trinidad, there is a considerable timbering industry, 641,485 cubic feet being cut for lumber in 1937 and 2,189,323 for corduroy and firewood. Port of Spain is an important trade center not only for the neighboring British Islands but also for the South American mainland and does an important business in reshipment as well as in the fueling of steamships with oil and coal.

Tobago's chief exports in 1938 were: cacao, $184,094; copra, $78,778; coconuts, $920. There was also a considerable shipment of foodstuffs to Trinidad.

Transportation and Communications

Because of the position of Trinidad on the southern route from Europe to northern Venezuelan and Colombian ports and the Panama Canal and the function that Port of Spain performs as a trade center, all of the many steamship lines running into the southern Caribbean make regular stops there. A deep-water harbor project, now nearly completed at Port of Spain at an estimated cost of £1,765,500 will provide a 3170-foot wharf wall with a depth of 30 feet below low water (later to be increased to 32 feet), an entrance channel 13,000 feet long, and a basin 4000 feet by 500 feet.

Through the Pan American Airways, Trinidad has regular passenger and mail connections with the United States, Mexico, the whole of the

Caribbean area, and both the east and west coasts of South America. Cable connections with the outside world are through the central stations on Barbados. Wireless communication is maintained with Barbados and with most of the islands of the Windward and Leeward Islands Colonies by Cable and Wireless, (West Indies), Ltd., while government stations at Port of Spain and North Post on Trinidad and at Scarborough on Tobago maintain communications with Martinique, British Guiana, Dutch Guiana, and Venezuela and with ships at sea.

Trinidad has 123 miles of standard-gauge railway, divided into three lines centering at Port of Spain and so located as to serve the most important producing sections of the country. A system of 1080 miles of main roads, of which all but 149 are metaled or graveled and oiled, permits motor transportation to practically all the important parts of the island. Tobago also has a fairly good system of roads suitable for motor traffic. Transportation between Trinidad and Tobago is carried on by coastal steamers operated by the government.

BRITISH GUIANA

Government. Executive Branch: Governor and Executive Council, appointed by the crown. Legislative branch: Legislative Council (Governor, Colonial Secretary, and Attorney General as ex-officio members, 10 official members, and 19 nonofficial members of whom 5 are nominated by the Governor and 14 elected unde a limited franchise.)

PHYSICAL FEATURES

British Guiana has an area of more than four times that of all the other British colonies in the Caribbean region combined, but of its 90,000 square miles only some 198 are under cultivation. Except for a few scattered ranches on the savanas in the mountainous southwestern part of the colony, the cultivated lands lie along the coast and up the lower reaches of the principal rivers.

The coast region is an alluvial plain, 25 to 40 miles wide east of the mouth of the Essequibo River but somewhat narrower to the west. Part of this plain lies below high-water level and is protected from invasion by the sea by an elaborate system of sea defenses originally constructed during the Dutch occupation. Along its inner edge stretches a broad undulating belt of sandy clays surmounted in places by lines of narrow dunes and shell deposits, marking a former coast line.

The Essequibo River and the other main streams farther east flow northward, following a gentle slope down from their headwaters at elevations of about 1200 feet along the southern boundary with Brazil. West of the Essequibo, however, the greater part of the area is drained by generally west-to-east flowing tributaries of the Essequibo. The Cuyuni and Mazaruni tributaries water a belt of hilly country about 120 miles wide which extends from within 50 miles of the coast to the steep scarp that fronts the

Pakaraima Range. This is the gold and diamond-bearing section of the colony.

Three parallel mountain systems cross the colony from west to east. The northernmost range, the Pakaraima, which reaches an elevation of 8635 feet in the famous Mt. Roraima, at the junction of British Guiana, Venezuela, and Brazil, is mainly a succession of terraces and broad plateaus with sheer sandstone escarpments. East of the Essequibo River it is continued by low hills. The highest peaks of the central range, which scarcely exceed 1600 feet, lie at its western end. The broad heavily forested Akarai Mountains, which carry the southern boundary of the colony with Brazil, have maximum elevations of less than 1500 feet. Of special interest from the standpoint of possible future settlement are the broad savana areas at elevations of 300 to 700 feet above sea level that border and separate these ranges.

The rivers provide the only highways between the interior and the coast, but except for small craft they are not navigable for more than about 50 miles inland from the sea. Beyond, because of numerous rapids, only canoe navigation is possible. On the sheer sandstone escarpments of the Pakaraima Range are many waterfalls. The Kaieteur Fall, with a vertical drop of 741 feet, is recognized as the highest single-drop waterfall in the world.

Except for the cultivated coastal zone, a triangular savana on the coast between Georgetown and the mouth of the Courantyne River, and savanas in the southwest, the whole colony is heavily forested. Commercially, the most important forest products are greenheart, rubber, balata, and oils and fat substitutes derived from many varieties of nut trees and palms.

Climate

In the coastal region the mean annual temperature is about 80.4° F., with the mean temperature for the warmest months (August, September, October) 82° F. and for the coolest months (January, February, March) 79° F. Temperatures of more than 89° F. are rare, even in the hottest months. There is considerable diurnal variation (12° to 14°): night temperatures average 72° to 74° F. and may on rare occasions fall as low as 70° F. during the coolest months. Breezes from the sea, generally from the northeast or east, blow steadily during the day throughout most of the year and in the coolest months continuously night and day. There are two wet and two dry seasons—a long wet season from the middle of April to the middle of August succeeded by a long dry season to the middle of November, and a shorter wet season from the middle of November to the end of January followed by a short dry season to the middle of April. The average annual rainfall at Georgetown, in Demerara County, is 91.6 inches and in the coastal section of Berbice, the next county to the east, 75 inches. In the forested interior day temperatures are higher than on the coast and night temperatures noticeably lower, while the rainfall is much heavier—as high as 130 to 140 inches annually. On the southwestern savanas, however, the rainfall is much lower than elsewhere (averaging 58.51 inches at Dadawana on the Rupununi River) and there is only one rainy season—May to September.

HISTORICAL NOTE

Although Columbus probably sighted the coast of what is now British Guiana he made no landing. Vicente Yañez de Pinzón is credited with having been the first to explore the coast and some of the rivers (1499 and 1500). British Guiana is the only British colony in the Caribbean region in whose early settlement the British had no real part and which at no time before the nineteenth century was recognized by international agreement as a British possession. The first permanent settlement was made by the Dutch West India Company in what is now Essequibo County about 1624. Colonization on any really large scale did not begin, however, until 1740, when the Dutch governor opened the banks of the lower Essequibo River to settlers from all countries and offered inducements of free land and ten years' freedom from taxes. The Demerara River was opened to settlement at about the same time, but it was not until 1763 that a colony was founded at the mouth of the Berbice River. During the following half century the three colonies were three times seized and held by the British (1781–1784, 1796–1802, 1803–1814) and were finally ceded to Great Britain by the Treaty of Paris of 1814.

POPULATION

The estimated population of British Guiana in 1938 was 337,221, of whom 3.2 per cent were of European origin (about four-fifths being of Portuguese descent), 42 per cent were East Indians (former indentured servants and their descendants), 12 per cent of mixed blood, 38 per cent Negroes, 2.6 per cent Indians, and 1 per cent Chinese. Georgetown, the capital, has an estimated population of 67,448 and New Amsterdam, the next town of importance, 9650. The birth rate in 1937 was 29.7 per 1000 and the death rate 31.9, both being considerably higher among the East Indians than any other racial group.

SOCIAL CONDITIONS

The chief employers of labor are the sugar estates. It is estimated that 69,600 persons were living on the 24 estates producing sugar in 1938 and that about 34,000 of these were employed. Some are also employed in growing rice and preparing it for the market, but the official reports give no indication of the number. Bauxite mining employed an average of about 1097 in 1938, and other mining industries (gold and diamonds) 1684. Road and water transport of all types engaged 2640 in 1931 (no later statistics). Balata collecting and wood cutting provide work for a small number—the former 568 in 1938. The total number of wage earners, regularly and intermittently employed, according to the 1931 census was 112,959, of which more than half were East Indians.

British Guiana is the most backward of all the British colonies in the Caribbean area from the standpoint of legislation for the welfare of the working class, and there is little government regulation respecting housing for workers, wages, working hours, medical care, or education. Practically all of this is left to the estate owner, whose arrangements for his labor force are almost entirely voluntary and gratuitous.

A large part of the housing provided on the estates is still the old barracks type of 20 to 30 rooms in a block and is in general quite unfit for occupation from any civilized point of view. Some progress has been made by a number of the estates in providing detached houses, and some of the laborers build their own houses on land rented or allotted to them. One of the most serious obstacles in the way of any attempt at improvement is the necessity in most sections of building the houses on piles because of the generally waterlogged and frequently flooded condition of the land; another is the archaic but widely prevalent system of dividing the land in long strips so narrow as to prohibit the construction of houses conforming to modern standards of space. Furthermore, the more valuable agricultural land lies along the coast, much of it below sea level. This necessitates the maintenance of an elaborate system of sea defense—dikes, canals, locks, sluices, and pumps—that was installed with slave labor when sugar was yielding high profits in a seemingly limitless market. In the face of declining markets, the tremendous burden that all this involves for both the government and the estates further restricts any efforts toward improvements in housing or increasing the number of small holdings.

The peasant proprietors and tenants, who form a large element in the population, are in a position to grow a large part of their own food, since their two main money crops, rice and sugar, require only intermittent attention; and the landless agricultural laborers are afforded opportunity to grow food crops on land allotted to them on the estates and to supplement their diet with wild and semiwild tree foods, to be had in many sections for the picking, as well as with fish, with which the sea and the canals are said to teem. There seems to be a rather larger consumption of milk than in any of the other colonies, but meat is expensive and must play a very small part in the diet of the laboring class. Estimates prepared by various labor unions in 1938 give the cost of living for town-dwelling laborers on a subsistence level as $1.50 a week exclusive of rent and offer a budget for a fairly ample diet at $3.00.

Figures are not available on the number of owners of small holdings. The census of 1931, however, reports a total of 74,603 engaged in agriculture, of whom 51,705 were laborers and 22,898 were classified as "landed proprietors, agriculturalists, cattle farmers." Since about 30 per cent of the total agricultural population belong to the latter class, it is evident that a large proportion of them must be small proprietors, tenants, and share croppers. None of these play a very important part in the cultivation of sugar cane, contributing only 1997 acres in 1938 to a total of 62,941 reaped. Rice growing is chiefly in the hands of the East Indians, to whom large areas on abandoned sugar estates are rented for the purpose. Coconuts and cacao are also produced mainly by small growers, although there are a few estates of fair size devoted to each. Much government land is available for purchase or long-term lease, but very little of it is in the coastal zone. Attention has been given to colonization possibilities in the southwest savana areas, but no development is to be expected there unless there is assurance that the agricultural potentialities of these areas are such as to warrant the building of a road or railroad connecting them with the coast.

PRODUCTION AND TRADE

Agricultural products account for more than two-thirds of the value of the colony's exports. The value of the sugar-cane products exported in 1938 (sugar, molasses, and rum), totaling $8,350,449, was more than 13 times that of all the other agricultural exports. Agricultural exports in 1938 were: sugar, $7,573,905; rice, $577,155; rum, $474,453; molasses, $302,091; coconut products (coconuts, copra, coconut oil), $48,585. Bauxite (export value in 1938, $2,046,793) is the second most important product. Gold exports in 1938 amounted to $1,044,305, diamonds to $381,984, timber to $351,375, balata to $185,867.

The sugar cane is now raised principally on 24 estates, and only a very small amount is supplied by small proprietors. In spite of the reduction of the area in cane by 8000 acres between 1928 and 1938, the production in 1938 was the highest on record (196,502 tons), owing to the fact that during the same period the yield per acre has been doubled by the introduction of new varieties of cane and improved methods of cultivation. The production of rice has declined considerably in recent years on account of unfavorable weather and low prices (exports in 1937, 18,765 tons; in 1938, 12,888), while the local consumption (24,000 tons) is increasing. Small quantities of coffee are exported (value in 1938, $5657), as well as of lime juice ($1860) and lime oil ($20,163).

What are believed to be very extensive deposits of manganese have recently been discovered by the Colony's Geological Survey between the Barima and Barama Rivers.

Manufacturing, except that connected with the sugar-cane industry, is of minor importance only. The refining of edible coconut oil is developing rapidly, however, under high tariff protection so that the importation in 1938 was only 123,380 gallons as compared with 144,350 gallons in 1932.

TRANSPORTATION AND COMMUNICATIONS

British Guiana has only two short lengths of railway along the coast, one running from Georgetown to the left bank of the Berbice River opposite New Amsterdam (60½ mi.) and the other from the left bank of the Demerara River opposite Georgetown to the mouth of the Essequibo River (18½ mi.).

There is a total of 272 miles of road passable for motor traffic in the coastal region. Transportation between the coastal region and the interior is chiefly by river boat. The Demerara, Essequibo, and Berbice Rivers are navigable for shallow-draft steamers for 90, 35, and 150 miles, respectively, but beyond these distances they are all interrupted by numerous rapids and falls and are navigable only by canoes. Several roads suitable for motor traffic have also been constructed into the interior but only for relatively short distances, the longest being from Bartica, the steamer terminus on the Essequibo River, to the headwaters of the Konawaruk tributary of the Essequibo (118 mi.). A cattle trail maintained by the government runs from the lower Berbice River to the Rupununi River (182 mi.).

In normal times the colony is served by British, French, and Dutch transatlantic steamship companies, by government steamships from Surinam, and by a number of United States and Canadian companies. A regular weekly air transport service to and from the United States and the east coast of South America is maintained by Pan American Airways.

There is a good telephone and telegraph network in the coastal zone, and a government-owned radio station affords communication with a number of stations in the interior and with the outside world.

BRITISH HONDURAS

Government. Executive branch: Governor and Executive Council (3 official members and such others—official or nonofficial—as may be appointed with the approval of the crown). Legislative branch: Legislative Council (Governor, 5 official members, 8 nonofficial members—2 nominated by the Governor, 6 elected under limited franchise).

PHYSICAL FEATURES

British Honduras, the only European possession on the mainland of Central America, has an area of about 8598 square miles, including 159 square miles in offshore islands and cays.

The northern half of the colony, north of the Sibun River, is a level country with many large lagoons, swamps, and sluggish rivers. The last are navigable for long distances by craft of shallow draft and provide the chief means of communication. The prevailing rock is limestone, but there are also large areas of so-called "pine ridges," composed of almost pure sand overlying sandstones and covered with a species of red pine. Although the best agricultural lands in this section are the alluvial soils along the rivers, tracts of good soil are found away from the rivers.

Southward from the headwaters of the Sibun and Belize Rivers the terrain back of the coastal lowlands is hilly. The main range, known as Maya Mountains, parallels the coast, rising to elevations of more than 2800 feet.

The hills are mostly of metamorphosed sandstone, although marbles, schists, and gneisses have been reported in the Cockscomb Mountains, a short east-running outlier of the Maya range, in which Victoria Peak (3700 feet) is the highest crest in the colony. The Belize River rises in pine-forested hills, immediately south of which are areas of oak and mahogany. In the extreme south, beyond the Deep River, there is a fertile rolling country underlain by folded calcareous sandstones. Extending from Belize south to Deep River, a low coastal plain of recent alluvial deposits averages about 8 or 10 miles in width and is much broken by lagoons and surmounted in places by sandy pine ridges similar to those farther north.

For a distance of 20 to 30 miles out to sea islands, cays, and coral reefs border the shore and shield it from the waves. They provide a number of safe harbors and roadsteads, but only south of Belize are these practicable for deep-draft steamers, and entrance to them is everywhere by narrow channels.

CLIMATE

Climatic conditions differ considerably in various parts of the colony because of differences in position and topography. Easterly winds prevail during the greater part of the year. The mean annual temperature at Belize is about 81° F., with the mean temperature of the hottest month (August) 83° F. and of the coolest month (January) 76° F. In the interior temperatures as high as 100° F. occur toward the end of the dry season (middle of February to the middle of May). The average monthly rainfall in the dry season is about two inches. October, November, and December are the rainiest months. The average annual fall increases from north to south— 50 inches at Corozal, 55 at El Cayo, 60 at Belize, 90 at Stann Creek, 100 at Middlesex, and 150 at Punta Gorda.

HISTORICAL NOTE

The coast of what is now British Honduras is believed to have been discovered by Columbus in 1502, and the first settlements are supposed to have been made in 1638 by adventurers from Jamaica who had come to exploit logwood. After frequent attempts to expel the English, the Spanish ceded the region to Great Britain in 1670. By 1713 there was an established government consisting of elected magistrates. The Spanish renewed their attempts to seize the colony, but by the Treaty of London of 1786 it was agreed between Great Britain and Spain that the former should be given possession of the area between the Belize and Sibun Rivers and also St. George's Cay in exchange for relinquishing her claim to the Mosquito Coast. Many Spaniards driven from Yucatan in 1849 by a revolt of the Indians settled in the northern part of the colony, and their settlements were repeatedly raided by the Yucatan Indians up to 1872.

The first constitution, granted by the king of England in 1765, gave the colonists the right to continue their custom of legislating by public meetings and of electing, by free suffrage of the people, magistrates to carry out all executive and judicial functions. In 1786, however, a superintendent appointed by the crown took over the administration of the colony, and government by elected magistrates was discontinued. The magistrate system was restored for a brief period from 1791 to 1797, but from that date until 1862, when the colony was placed in control of a lieutenant governor subordinate to the governor of Jamaica, superintendents were again in charge. It was not until 1884 that the colony was made independent of Jamaica.

POPULATION

The population of British Honduras was estimated in 1938 as 57,767 (about 6 per square mile), of which less than 4 per cent were white, about 48 per cent Negro and mixtures of Negro and other bloods, 24 per cent Maya Indian, 8 per cent Carib, and the remaining 16 per cent chiefly Spanish and Spanish and Indian mixtures from Mexico and the neighboring Central American countries. More than half the population lives in towns. Belize, the capital and chief town, has about 16,687 inhabitants, the other important towns, according to the 1931 census, being Stann Creek (2844), Corozal (2197), El Cayo (1260), Bengue Viejo (1211), Punta Gorda (1119), Orange Walk (1099). The birth rate in 1938 was 35.5 per 1000, the death rate 20.3.

SOCIAL CONDITIONS

The number of individual holdings of agricultural land is reported as fairly high in relation to the total population and must be when it is considered that the total force of laborers depending entirely on wage earning was estimated at only 6000 in 1938. Moreover, although there are no very large agricultural estates, the holdings of small proprietors are much larger than elsewhere in the British Caribbean colonies, even the native planters often owning from 10 to 300 acres. Crown land can be rented at about 30 cents an acre or bought for $2 to $3 an acre, but most of it is now rather inaccessible. There seems, however, to be no great desire on the part of the laboring element to take up land, and when they do they are apt to gamble on an export crop rather than to practice subsistence farming or the growing of food crops for the town markets.

With so large a proportion of the population living in towns there is much overbuilding and overcrowding of houses. Building standards are in general extremely low. In Belize, for example, groups of small tenement houses packed together in the backyards of better-class houses are characteristic. Much of the housing in Belize, owing to the swampy and often flooded condition of the land, is on piles. The general practice in the timber industry is for the men to build their own huts at the beginning of each cutting season.

In the towns the food of all classes is largely imported; in the agricultural districts the permanent occupants grow little in the way of food but devote themselves to raising export crops; and even the timber workers who are rurally domiciled make no practice of growing food crops during the off season. Everywhere except among the Indians polished rice of inferior quality is preferred to the superior local product, white flour to locally produced corn meal, evaporated and condensed milk to fresh milk, and salt pork from the United States to fresh meat, which could be raised locally in sufficient quantity to supply the population. Even the limited quantities of fresh vegetables consumed come mostly from outside the colony.

Of the 6000 laborers depending solely on wage earning, about 14 per cent were employed in mahogany cutting, 16 per cent in chicle gathering, 16 per cent in agriculture, and more than half in general labor, domestic service, and construction trades.

In general, wages appear to be considerably higher than in the other British colonies in the Caribbean area, but employment is largely seasonal, and the ordinary laborer seems to have no ability to save enough to tide himself over the annual period of unemployment. As the mahogany and chicle workers in general make no effort to supplement their wages by growing food crops during the slack period, it follows that the laborers are usually reduced almost, if not quite, to destitution before the season opens again. The government practices a system of rotating labor on public works in an effort to relieve this situation to some extent.

PRODUCTION AND TRADE

Forest products (mainly mahogany and chicle but some cedar, rosewood, and logwood) are the most important exports of British Honduras, with a total value in 1938 of $1,369,460. Other exports in 1938 were: bananas, $282,890; grapefruit, $84,423; and coconuts, $49,803. The sugar production averages about 1500 tons and is not sufficient for local use, $53,000 worth having been imported in 1938. Some rum of rather inferior quality and molasses, both for local consumption, are produced. The local need beyond that met by local production was formerly largely supplied by refined and raw sugar from Guatemala and Honduras, but, as the result of preferential tariffs within the British Commonwealth, it now comes from the British West Indies. Mahogany is cut both from privately owned forests and crown lands. Bananas for a number of years have been the principal agricultural product, and, although many of the banana-growing areas are infected now with disease to a rather alarming degree (exports in 1938 amounted to $47,201 less than in 1937), they are still the favorite money crop of both the large and the small proprietors. Twenty years ago coconut growing was the most important agricultural industry in the colony, and the plantations form an almost continuous fringe along the coast and on the cays, but exports have declined rapidly owing to low prices and shortage of efficient shipping facilities. Grapefruit production on the other hand is increasing rapidly, the total export value in 1938 being more than double that of any previous year. Rice and corn are still grown under the *milpa* (shifting agriculture) system, mostly by small planters. The production of neither is sufficient for local consumption, although it might easily be. Areas in rice, however, were considerably increased in 1938, partly because of the decline in banana production and partly because of the encouragement offered by the erection of rice mills and purchases of rice at good prices by the Board of Agriculture of the colonial government. Cattle are raised chiefly to supply working animals for hauling mahogany, although there seems to be no reason why sufficient beef cattle should not be grown to supply at least the demands of the local market. In fact, the indications are that both the variety and quantity of agricultural products could be very much increased.

Transportation and Communications

There is passenger, mail, and freight service by United States fruit company lines weekly between Belize and New Orleans by way of Puerto Barrios (Guatemala), about once a week by way of Jamaica and Cuba, and direct about once a month by United Fruit Company ships. The Canadian National line affords service between Montreal or Halifax and Belize fortnightly by way of Kingston (Jamaica), Nassau, and Bermuda. In normal times a British line from Liverpool and a Dutch line from Amsterdam, sailing by way of the West Indies, call about once a month.

Weekly mail and passenger service by air are provided by Mexican and Central American companies, through Mexico to the United States and to various points in Central America, where connection can be made for North and South America by the Pan American Airways.

Cable connection with the outside world is made by a cable to Chetumal, across the boundary in Mexico, and then by way of cables serving that country. A wireless station at Belize provides radiotelegraph communication through stations in Jamaica, at Guatemala City, and at New Orleans.

Internal communication is chiefly by boat and pack trail, although the principal towns are connected by passenger and freight air service furnished by the Compania de Transportes Aereos Centro-Americanos (Taca). Motor roads are now under construction from Punta Gorda in the Toledo District to the Indian town of San Antonio—a total length of 21 miles, of which 17 were open to traffic in 1938—and 84 miles were open to motor traffic in 1938 of a 99-mile road from Belize to Corozal by way of Orange Walk. The 25-mile railway running inland from Commerce Bight in the Stann Creek District, the only railway in the country, is now being converted into a road. A telegraph system connects the principal towns, and there is a small telephone system that operates both independently and in connection with the telegraph system.

THE FRENCH COLONIES

The French West Indies consist of three colonies: Martinique, Guadeloupe and its dependencies, and French Guiana. Guadeloupe and Martinique are distinguished from both the Netherlands and the British type of colony in the Caribbean area in that they have elected representation in both houses of the French Parliament and their local legislative assemblies are elected by universal manhood suffrage. In French Guiana, although one deputy is elected to the French Parliament, suffrage is limited to resident French citizens. The French island, Clipperton, which lies in the Pacific Ocean about 500 miles west of Costa Rica, is also included in this section because it is frequently mentioned in connection with the defense of the Panama Canal.

MARTINIQUE

Government. Executive branch: Governor assisted by a Privy Council (composed of the Secretary General, the Chief of the Judiciary Service, the Commander of the Troops, and two other councilors). Legislative branch: General Council (36 members elected by universal suffrage). Representation in French Parliament: one senator and two deputies.

PHYSICAL FEATURES

Martinique (area: about 385 sq. mi.) is a rugged volcanic island formed on a platform of ancient crystalline rocks that have been covered by marine sediments and later overlaid with lava and other material from numerous volcanic centers. The mountains are generally steep, with knife-edge ridges and deep ravines. The island may be divided into three physiographic regions, each dominated by a central massif. With their connecting ranges these form the backbone of the island. The southern region, culminating in the Massif de Vauclin (1657 feet), is the lowest of the three. The central region, although it does not contain the highest peak, is the most extensive elevated area. Its core, the Pitons de Carbet, is distinguished by four extremely steep, pinnacle-like mountains of which the highest rises to 3960 feet. The northern region is completely dominated by Mont Pelée (4428 feet), a steep volcanic cone with a huge base occupying the whole northern end of the island.

There is little level land, except for the Plain of Lamentin extending along the Bay of Fort-de-France on the southwest side of the island and small patches between some of the ravines and in crescentic areas along the coasts.

The rivers are generally short, rushing torrents that roar down to the sea after mountain rains and eventually dwindle to mere trickles, some of which disappear altogether during the dry season. The eastward-flowing rivers (20 in number) have the more regular flow because they are on the windward side where there is more rainfall and where the vegetation helps to prevent an excessively rapid runoff. The 21 westward-flowing rivers, however, are more important because they cross the drier part of the island.

The southern two-thirds of the east coast and the entire coast line south of the Bay of Fort-de-France are low, irregular, and rocky or swampy (as along the Plain of Lamentin). Here the coastal waters are shallow. Wave-washed coral reefs and islets and, on the east, the trade winds make these shores dangerous to approach. Off the northwest and north coasts the water is very deep near shore. At the north end of the island there are great cliffs three hundred feet high separated by small, deeply cut valleys.

Climate

Four seasons have been recognized in Martinique: January 15 to April 15, cool and dry; April 15 to July 15, warm and relatively dry; July 15 to October 15, hot and humid with storms and heavy rain; October 15 to January 15, rainy and cool. The island is ravaged by hurricanes about once in every ten years. Most of these occur in September, though occasionally they come in August, October, or late July.

The insular situation keeps the temperature even. The easterly winds from over the Atlantic are fresh, cooling, and moisture-laden, but, during the dreaded calm spells in spring and summer and in places entirely cut off from breezes, the heat and humidity may become almost unbearable. The mean annual temperature at Fort-de-France is 79.2° F. The seasonal temperature range is very slight (4° to 5° F.), the diurnal range being much greater. The coolest month, January, averages 76.1° F. and the warmest month, May, 80.9° F., but the late summer and early fall months are much more unpleasant than May because of humidity and calm spells.

There are clouds over Martinique most all the time with the possible exception of early morning. The relative humidity averages 80 per cent. February, March, April, and May have the least humidity with 76 to 78 per cent, while the fall of the year averages 82 to 83 per cent.

In general, Martinique is rainy but has a dry season from January to July. November is the month of maximum rainfall. The mean annual rainfall for the wettest station, Deux Choux in the north-central part, is 220.09 inches, falling in approximately 285 rainy days. The driest station, Diamant, on the extreme southwestern coast, has 41.68 inches in approximately 125 rainy days. The two highest and wettest areas, around Mont Pelée and the Pitons de Carbet, receive more than 190 inches a year and are encircled by concentric belts of diminishing rainfall. The high year-round temperature, the rapid evaporation rate, and the porosity of the volcanic deposits, which allows a rapid penetration of the water, make the southern section semiarid to arid in spite of its 41-inch rainfall.

Natural Vegetation

The original vegetation has to a large extent been destroyed by man, volcanic activity, and storms. Only 20 to 22 per cent of the island remains in natural vegetation.

The tropical rain forest, characterized by palms, bamboo, and a large number of monocotyledonous plants and lianas, occupies the deep ravines and the lower mountain slopes in the northern part of the island at altitudes generally below 1000 feet. The mass of this vegetation is almost impenetrable and largely precludes any use being made of the land. The subtropical rain forest, at altitudes between 1000 and 2500 feet, is characterized by beautiful tree ferns and certain species of rhododendron and magnolia. Above 2500 feet there is a zone of temperate grasslands, exposed to the cool moist trade winds and with almost continuous rain and cloud cover. Lichens, hardy grasses, bracken, small ferns, and dwarf woody bushes grow on the steep slopes. Much of this area is used for grazing.

The drought-resistant types of vegetation include thorn forests and a cactus low-bush, low-tree association. The thorn forests, comprising acacia, bayehonde, and campeche, are found along almost the entire western coast line and in the low-lying northern part of the southwestern peninsula. The cactus low-bush, low-tree area occupies much of the dry southern part of the island south of the central divide. The characteristic plants are dwarf algarroba trees, cacti, and agaves. The south coast and interior of the southern peninsula is a thorny bushland, devoted largely to grazing and very sparsely populated.

Salt-tolerant plants occur along most of the coast line but especially along the southwest and east coasts. The seaward edge of the Plain of Lamentin is covered by a mixture of low mangroves, acacias, and salt grasses, and there are numerous small tracts of mangroves and swamp grass along the southeast coast.

Practically all lumber for houses, shipbuilding, etc. is imported. The United States has shipped most of the lumber, but recently some has come from France. Although the forests of Martinique are lacking in great commercial value, they are necessary to the island's welfare because they prevent floods and landslides, help regulate the streams, and enrich the soil. Martinique would be better off if the forests had not been so completely destroyed in the southern and central parts of the island.

With the exception of the marsh areas and the tops of some of the steep mountains, there is little natural grassland in Martinique suitable for grazing purposes.

HISTORICAL NOTE

Although Martinique was discovered by Columbus in 1502, while on his fourth voyage, the Spaniards did not settle the island because it lacked the gems and precious metals they had hoped to find. After colonization by the French in 1635, there was a 50-year formative period, during which the struggling settlement suffered from wars with the Caribs, English, and Dutch, from internal revolts, and from ruinous treatment by the various rulers. Snakes and disease added to the troubles. The introduction of sugar and slavery in the late 1600's ushered in a new period of plantation development, which lasted until the abolition of slavery in 1848, though broken by many wars and natural disasters. French sovereignty over the island has been uncontested since 1816. During the World War, Martinique had 40,000 men serving in France, and the colony did all it could to supply cacao, sugar, and rum to the mother country.

In the 305-year life of the colony, there have been 33 hurricanes, 7 earthquakes (one with 232 shocks in one series of 5 years), 5 serious fires, 2 famines, 1 drought, 11 storms with tidal waves, and 3 volcanic eruptions, one of which, the eruption of Mont Pelée in 1902, wiped out approximately 30,000 people and completely destroyed one of the greatest cities in the Caribbean and the world's greatest rum-exporting center. Martinique has averaged a disaster every 4¾ years and has been through 19 wars.

POPULATION

From 1635 to 1939–1940 the population of Martinique increased from 100 to 241,000. In the last one hundred years the population has been more than doubled, a gain that is remarkable in view of a very high infant-mortality rate until recently and a death rate that has always been high because of natural disasters, fevers, and other tropical diseases. During the period 1895–1905 economic difficulties and the destruction of Saint Pierre led to a recession in the population trend, and a slight falling off has occurred in the last four or five years. There are, on an average, 615 persons to the square mile, but because of the character of the land surface and its utilization, the distribution of population is uneven. The density must be approximately 1000 to the square mile in some parts of the island and less than 50 in others.

The original colonists were all white indentured servants, criminals, debtors, and adventurers, who managed practically to exterminate the Indians in 23 years and thus make the population dominantly white. After the introduction of slaves to work in the sugar fields, it became largely Negro (more than 60 per cent of the people were slaves in 1842). The mixed or mulatto population that prevails today is due to mixed marriages and more or less unchecked promiscuity. After the slaves were freed in 1848, many of the planters were unable to get sufficient labor, because the freed people preferred an independent life in the hills, and in order to provide labor about 25,000 Hindus were imported. Many of these eventually returned to India or died, but some of their descendants remain on the island. With the Hindus came some Chinese and Annamites. There are also a few Syrians. The white population, largely French, now numbers between three and four thousand, and there is also a very small group of foreign whites.

The first settlements were made on the leeward west coast, where small bays offer quiet anchorages and protected fishing grounds. The deltas and low-lying coastal valleys were utilized for farm land, while the mountain streams provided fresh water. The difficulties of penetrating the interior kept the planters close to the coast. However, the lowlands were soon occupied, and the freed slaves, freed indentured workers, and small colonists had to seek the hills.

Most of the people of Martinique are rural and live in subsistence settlements. There is only one large urban center, Fort-de-France and its suburbs, where more than twenty per cent of the population is concentrated. The three principal areas of habitation are along the west-central coast north of the Bay of Lamentin, in the central mountain district, and along all of the east coast with the exception of the southern tip. The rest of the island is sparsely inhabited: in the north Mont Pelée has destroyed most of the potential resources; the north-central mountain area is too wet, too densely forested, and too steep; and the southeastern and southern parts are too dry. The Plain of Lamentin is so valuable for sugar that there is little space for human habitation.

The agglomerated settlements, other than Fort-de-France, are of four types: coastal sugar towns, fishing villages, interior subsistence towns, and interior sugar towns. Most of the smaller settlements are on the coast or on river banks near the coast.

SOCIAL CONDITIONS

Although it is difficult and dangerous to generalize, it may be said that the people of Martinique as a whole are friendly, intelligent, and much more industrious than the people of the majority of the West Indian islands.

Fortunately the balance of trade has been more or less favorable, thanks to the connection with France, and there has been considerable money in the island, though most of the money and land is in the hands of a very few. The wealthy white planters, who virtually own the island, number about 1000. The middle class consists of officials, gendarmes, merchants, technical employees in the sugar mills, and a few dozen professional men, about 2000 in all. Field laborers make up most of the rest of the population.

Although there has been unemployment, it has not been serious until recently, partly because so many of the people live on subsistence farms in the hills and partly because the terrain is so hilly that hand labor is necessary on almost all the plantations. In recent years, however, Martinique has been faced with the problem of a generally increasing population and a decreasing value of sugar. Almost all the arable land is under cultivation, there is no opportunity for expansion, and the inevitable problem of unemployment is becoming acute. Field hands are paid by the amount of work accomplished—for example, about 13 francs for cutting a ton of cane. Technical men in the mills receive about 20 to 30 francs a day.

Strikes have been attempted to force the large planters to pay higher wages, but so far they have not been very successful because there is such a large poor agricultural population that is anxious to work.

Most of the people live in the transition zone between the lowlands and the mountains on hand-cleared subsistence plots of a quarter of an acre to two acres. The rural houses are one or two-room shacks about ten or twelve feet wide by twenty feet long. Some of them are made of local materials such as bamboo and small branches, but most of them are built with nondescript boards, many of which look as if they came from old packing cases. The roofs are made of sugar-cane refuse, bamboo, and other thatch materials; when tile or, more rarely, sheet iron is used, it is a sign of affluence. The floors are generally bare earth. The windows are holes, which may be boarded up, since window glass is scarce. The interior furnishings are simple hand-made stools and chairs, though the interiors are surprisingly pleasing. Eating utensils vary from gasoline cans to dishes. In the towns the buildings are usually of stone with tile roofs. The diet of the poor agricultural laborers is dominantly starchy, with such subsistence products as yams, potatoes, breadfruit, manioc, and bananas. However, some fish, meat, poultry, mangoes, coconuts, and a few pineapples vary the diet. Owing to the cost of transporting food from the interior of the island, living costs are higher in the towns. During the present crisis the diet must be severely curtailed.

Although there have not been any government housing projects, agriculture has been promoted by a technical service. An agricultural credit bank was established to loan small farmers money; the interest rates run from 5 to 8 per cent and repayments may be made in installments.

The fact that almost all the land and wealth is under the control of a few families has retarded development of the population as a whole. Although the cost of living is generally low, money is difficult to accumulate because of the low value of agricultural crops and the abundance of manual labor. There is little opportunity for the average laborer to get ahead or to save enough money to leave the island, and the per-capita consumption of rum, estimated at a minimum of six gallons a year, is tremendous. The people are intensely loyal to France; and in spite of their nearness to English colonies and American republics they have not been attracted to the American sphere.

PRODUCTION

As there are no commercially valuable minerals, metals, or fuels in Martinique, the island is completely dependent upon agriculture. Three types of agriculture are practiced: commercial, secondary, and subsistence. Commercial agriculture, today almost the only remaining source of revenue, is conducted on the large plantations. Secondary agriculture, concerned with the growth of cash crops of a minor or local value, is of little economic importance. Subsistence farming yields products for home consumption.

Martinique produced 54,130 tons of sugar in 1938–1939 on 34,594 acres and exported approximately 46,565 tons, or a small fraction of one per cent of the world's sugar exports. Sugar was introduced from Brazil in

1654 and by 1700 had become the most important product. Today it is still the greatest crop, occupying the largest amount of agricultural land and providing work for more people than does anything else on the island. There are 20 sugar mills and 170 rum distilleries. The cane is grown chiefly on the windward northeast coast and in the low, west-central section of the island, with scattered plantations in mountain basins and on delta lands at the mouths of small streams on the leeward coast. The cane grown in limited amounts in the more remote areas is used in the local rum distilleries.

With 40 per cent of the area devoted to sugar cane and grasslands and with such great economic dependence on sugar, it might be assumed that the conditions for the growth of the crop were ideal. Unfortunately this is not the case. One difficulty is the lack of level land. With the exception of the Plain of Lamentin, some of the river valleys, and the coastal fringe, the island is too rugged and steep for plantation development. Furthermore, the planters cannot select the land that will produce the best cane but are forced to plant on any land that will grow cane, whatever its quality.

Climatically Martinique is somewhat better suited to sugar production than it is physiographically. The average annual temperature of 79.2° F. is ideal. Most of the rain, however, falls in rugged mountainous areas that cannot be planted in cane, and much of the lowland area is too dry. A short dry season is needed for commercial sugar production, but in Martinique the dry season lasting from February through May is too long, and some areas receive less than 2 inches of rain a month during this period.

Since the soils of Martinique and the type of cane established there preclude the production of a sugar as pure as that obtained elsewhere, Martinique sugar cannot favorably compete in the world market and is better used for rum production. Martinique rum has established a reputation especially in France, where it leads in the colonial rum quota. The export of rum from Martinique in 1938 was 4,623,543 gallons.

Comparatively recently sugar planters have introduced bananas. These have had a good start and a rapid growth, and today in most of the well watered parts of the island there are scattered spots where bananas are grown. A French refrigerated ship has been making regular calls to carry the bananas to France, where there has been an increasing demand for them. Although this industry is promising as a source of new wealth, it is still in its infancy. Martinique, however, is one of the lesser French banana-producing areas and meets but a very small part of the demand in the world market. Some pineapples have also been introduced.

Many secondary crops are cultivated, but, with very few exceptions, have not been successful except for brief periods. Coffee, cacao, cotton, vanilla have all been grown but have declined because of poor handling of the crops. Pests, natural disasters, and falling prices have caused much distress and discouragement, and there is an apparent lack of interest in any product but sugar. Except for 5 out of 21 products exported by Martinique, the record has been that of a brief rise and then a decline. Of the 5 products, sugar and rum are the only ones that have maintained their importance. Pineapples and bananas are relatively recent developments and are still rising. Cacao production today amounts to a little less than it did 115 years ago.

TRADE

During the years immediately preceding the present war, exports from Martinique have tended to exceed imports in value. In 1938, for example, the exports were valued at 309,648,000 francs as against imports valued at 227,332,000. The exports in that year consisted of the following principal commodities: sugar (144,989,000), rum (106,630,000), bananas (46,752,-000), pineapples (6,235,000), others (5,042,000). Nearly all the exports have gone to France. Of the imports, which consist of a wide variety of foods and beverages and of raw and manufactured products for local consumption, about two-thirds (in terms of value) came from France during the five-year period 1934–1938. In 1936 the value of the imports from France was about 65 per cent and of those from the United States about 15 per cent of the total value.

The colonial relationship to the mother country has been valuable to Martinique because it has assured a market for the island's most important products. The policy, nevertheless, has been dangerous and short-sighted, as the present crisis has shown. For its commercial existence the island has depended mostly upon one crop, sugar, and one country, France. Since sugar markets with a few exceptions are closed or protected, the prosperity of Martinique has been based upon a tropical commodity overproduced as far as the world is concerned. Not counting St. Pierre and Miquelon, France has only tropical colonies, all capable of producing almost the same products, and, in order to support these colonies, she has had to adopt a colonial quota system. Thus, although Martinique has been an outlet for some French manufactured goods and colonial enterprises and was a great reserve for rum and chocolate during crises like the World War, it certainly cannot be considered commercially essential to France as long as she retains such regions as Madagascar, Indo-China, and French Equatorial Africa.

Furthermore, with an economy geared to dependence upon sugar and its by-products, Martinique does not grow enough food to feed its own people and has to import almost everything it uses, including fish and even coffee and cacao. During late August, 1940, the British West Indian fleet blockaded several French submarines and cruisers and an aircraft carrier at the naval and air base of Fort-de-France, thus causing not only a military and diplomatic crisis but much hardship for the inhabitants of the island who were caught without adequate food and supplies.

Transportation and Communications

The roads of Martinique are good considering the difficulty of maintaining any road system in a steep rainy region where floods, landslides,
and mud hamper communications. There are 45 different roads totaling
332.5 miles. Almost all of these are usable by automobiles. The Fort-de-
France–St. Pierre road is a paved first-class road. Motor busses carry
passengers and mail to almost all parts of the island and there are several
small mail and passenger boats which connect the ports. Telephone connection is maintained to all parts of the island. With approximately 10
steamship lines and some 560 ships touching there yearly, Martinique in
peace times was well connected with the rest of the world, but since
August, 1940, most of the steamship lines have discontinued or curtailed
their services. Martinique may be reached via Pan American Airways
from Miami.

There are no good natural harbors except at Fort-de-France. The Bay
of St. Pierre used to be a good harbor but has been filled and shallowed by
the eruptions of Mont Pelée and is not safe for large ships on account of
the submerged and unmarked hulks of the vessels destroyed in the disaster
of 1902. The harbor of Fort-de-France is slowly being filled in with alluvial material but is large and well protected. The French have dredged a
channel and developed docks and a small navy yard where French naval
vessels and the French Line vessels can dock and, if necessary, be repaired.

GUADELOUPE AND DEPENDENCIES

Government. Executive branch: Governor and Privy Council (composed of the
Secretary General, the Procuror General, and two other councilors). Legislative
branch: General Council (36 members elected by universal suffrage). Representation in French Parliament: one senator and two deputies.

Areas

Guadeloupe and its dependencies (total area *ca.* 690 sq. mi.) consist of
the double island of Guadeloupe (583 sq. miles); the nearer dependencies,
Marie-Galante (58 sq. mi.), Désirade (14.5 sq. mi.), Petite-Terre (1.5
sq. mi.), and Les Saintes (5.5 sq. mi.), which form a small archipelago of
11 islands and numerous reefs and islets lying within a radius of about
twenty miles to the east, southeast, and south of Guadeloupe; and also
St. Barthélemy (St. Bartholomew; 8.3 sq. mi.), 75 miles northwest of
Guadeloupe, and the French part of the neighboring island of St. Martin
(20 sq. mi.).

GUADELOUPE

Physical Features

Guadeloupe proper (583 sq. mi.), is actually composed of two islands,
Basse-Terre (364 sq. mi.) to the west and Grande-Terre (219 sq. mi.) to

the east, separated by a mangrove swamp and a narrow tidal channel but linked by a bridge and a road over the swamp.

Basse-Terre is high, rugged, and volcanic, second only to Dominica in elevation among the Lesser Antillean islands. The old volcanoes, which average almost 3000 feet in altitude, have been much eroded and are dissected by deep ravines. Mt. Soufrière (4867 feet), the highest, is apparently dying or dormant but has several fumaroles and hot sulphur springs. The coast line of Basse-Terre is varied, with great cliffs, swamps, sandy beaches, and numerous indentations, but no good harbors. Even at the town of Basse-Terre, the capital, ships must anchor off shore.

Grande-Terre is very different. Formed of thick beds of limestone deposited on an ancient, eroded volcanic base, the island has a maximum elevation of about 400 feet, and its surface is generally level.

There are some coral reefs around both islands, especially Grande-Terre. The principal port and most important commercial city, Pointe-à-Pitre, is in Grande-Terre, on the Petit Cul-de-Sac, the southern of the two bays that separate Basse-Terre from Grande-Terre.

There are many torrential streams on Basse-Terre, some of them flowing through deep ravines with numerous falls. On Grande-Terre rivers are lacking because of the dryness, low elevation, and permeable limestone, although some ravines have been cut in the limestone and streams flow through them during the hard rains. In the dry months the inhabitants of Grande-Terre are obliged to collect water in cisterns.

CLIMATE

The average sea-level temperature in Guadeloupe is 79° F. The coolest month is February (74.8°), and July and August are the warmest (81.8°). The highest recorded temperature at Pointe-à-Pitre is 90.5° (July), and the lowest 61° (February). There is little difference in temperature from place to place on Grande-Terre, but on Basse-Terre the mountains are considerably cooler than the lower levels (Camp Jacob, at 1738 feet, has an average year-round temperature of 71°). Basse-Terre is wet, with 72 inches of rain falling annually at sea level even on the leeward coast and 204 inches at Camp Jacob, where there are 290 rainy days on an average each year. Some of the higher mountain peaks are nearly always cloud-covered and rainy. By contrast, Grande-Terre is relatively dry, with an average of only 69 inches of rainfall yearly. On both islands the rainiest months are in the fall and the driest period runs from December through April. The winds are generally from the northeast and east during the winter and from east and southeast, with frequent calms and variable breezes, during the summer. There is a hot wet season from May to November and a warm dry season from November to April.

VEGETATION

In general the wet and mountainous Basse-Terre is densely forested, so much so that very little use can be made of the central mountain core. Grande-Terre, on the other hand, is cultivable, most of the forest having been cleared away. There are three principal vegetation zones: lowlands, from sea level to about 1650 feet; uplands, from 1650 to about 3000 feet; and summit areas, above 3000 feet. The lowlands, which include the lower parts of Basse-Terre and all of Grande-Terre, are characterized by acacia, campeche, and other thorny trees typical of semiarid tropical regions, and mangrove swamps are found along the coasts. On the leeward side of Basse-Terre and in the limestone areas of Grande-Terre, grasses, cactuses, and agaves prevail. The uplands of Basse-Terre are covered by what is practically an equatorial rain forest, very dense and beautiful, with a tremendous number of different species of plants. Although some virgin forest remains in this zone, most of it has been destroyed by hurricanes or cut over for lumber and clearings. Where the cleared spots have been allowed to revert to nature, a modified tropical rain forest has resulted. The steep, wet, windy summits are mostly covered with low, heathlike plants and occasional stunted trees.

HISTORICAL NOTE

Although Columbus visited Guadeloupe on his second voyage and the islands were claimed for the king of Spain, the Spaniards found more profitable regions elsewhere and made no effort at colonization. The first French settlement, of 550 persons, was established in 1635. After a period of private ownership, Colbert purchased the islands for the French West India Company in 1664. From then on the colony rapidly developed into a great sugar-producing area. It was frequently attacked by the British, who occupied Guadeloupe eight different times up to 1816. Since then it has been continuously French.

POPULATION

The population of Guadeloupe is 304,239, with a density of 442.06 persons to the square mile. Pointe-à-Pitre is the largest center, with 43,551 inhabitants. The capital, Basse-Terre, has only 13,638.

Shortly after the arrival of the Breton, Norman, and Gascon colonists in 1635, the native Caribs were killed off or driven away, and many Negro slaves were imported from Africa. Thus the numerically predominant population changed in a relatively short time from Indian to European and then to Negro. At the present time most of the people are mulattoes, with a large Negro minority. Guadeloupe has a larger white population than Martinique, partly because it is the administrative center of the French West Indies.

In the late eighteenth century, the capital city, Basse-Terre, lost its commercial and numerical supremacy to Pointe-à-Pitre, largely because the latter is closer to the centers of sugar-cane production on Grande-Terre and has a much better harbor. With the exception of the capital, Pointe-à-Pitre, and the wave-swept east-coast port of Moule, there are no important towns. On Grande-Terre there are about a dozen coastal settlements and also many small centers near the sugar plantations and factories. On Basse-Terre almost all the villages lie on little bays along the coast, where fishing supplements subsistence agriculture, although a belt of subsistence farms and secondary cultures—broadest in the east-central part of the island—extends all the way around the island along the slopes of the higher mountains and supports a fairly dense population.

In general the standard of living is low. As in most of the other Lesser Antilles, the population is made up mostly of agricultural laborers, and there are few opportunities for social or economic advancement. Generally speaking social conditions are much the same as in Martinique.

PRODUCTION

Guadeloupe is completely dependent on agriculture. The great plantations have grown sugar from earliest times, with rum as a by-product. On Grande-Terre the temperatures, the level surface, and the limestone soils are well suited to sugar cane, which occupies 38 square miles, or about one fifth of the surface of that island, producing in 1938 45,328 metric tons of sugar for export, valued at 125,343,000 francs. In the same year 3,048,382 gallons of rum were manufactured, valued at 71,705,000 francs. The cane is harvested during the dry season, generally in January, when the sugar content is highest and the cool, dry weather is favorable for working in the fields. The dry climate and also damage from storms account in part for the relatively low yield of about 40 tons an acre, as compared with 60 tons in Java and 80 in Hawaii. There are about a dozen factories on Grande-Terre, each capable of handling between four and six thousand tons of sugar a year.

Basse-Terre does not have enough flat land for cane production on a large scale, but physical conditions are favorable for growing bananas, coffee, cacao, and vanilla. About 26 square miles were devoted to the first three in 1937. All of these crops, except coffee, require a high rainfall. Bananas grow well at low altitudes on the alluvial soils of the deltas just inland from the windward coast, but high winds, by breaking or uprooting the trees, may ruin a banana crop, whereas a crop of cane is much less likely to be completely destroyed. In spite of the setback of the severe hurricane of 1929, exports of bananas have greatly increased since 1926, reaching in 1938 50,287 metric tons, valued at 86,126,000 francs.

Cacao requires year-round warmth, humidity, shade, and shelter from storms. Through natural disasters, lack of proper care, and pests, many of the West Indian islands have lost their cacao exports, and today the Caribbean area is far behind the Guinea coast and Nigeria in the production of cacao. In 1938 Guadeloupe produced for export 134 metric tons valued at 595,000 francs, but in favorable years in the past it has exported an average of 900 metric tons. In the Vieux-Habitants area on the west-central coast of Basse-Terre there have been very large yields of cacao to the acre. Higher prices and proper development might make Guadeloupe into an important cacao-producing region once more.

Coffee is generally grown at elevations of about 2000 feet, the principal coffee-producing areas being in the interior subsistence districts of Basse-Terre. Thriving on well drained volcanic soil and requiring a short dry season and protection from winds, it does well in some of the hilly sections. Nevertheless, exports of coffee have declined along with almost all the other exports of the islands except sugar, rum, and bananas. In 1938 327 metric tons of coffee were exported, valued at 3,773,000 francs.

Conditions are favorable for the growth of pineapples, but the industry is young and the production small. In 1936, exports of vanilla and vanillon amounted to 128 metric tons.

TRADE

In general the balance of trade of Guadeloupe has been favorable. Thus in 1937, the exports of the islands were valued at 336,249,000 francs and the imports at 245,720,000 francs.

Guadeloupe is dependent on its exports of sugar, rum, and bananas and to some extent on its rapidly declining exports of coffee, cacao, and vanilla, but in world trade its products are insignificant—only a small fraction of one per cent of the world's traffic in these commodities.

Almost all the exports go to France and the French colonies. Commodities to the value of only 5,438,000 francs, or about 4 per cent of the total, were exported to countries other than France or her colonies in 1936, and these were mostly in the form of re-exported goods coming as ballast in various ships. Vanilla to the value of 714,000 francs was exported to the United States.

Most of the imports also come from France (82,849,000 francs worth, or about 66 per cent, in 1936, for example): oil, gasoline, wood, prepared foods, textiles, and manufactured products in general. The French colonies supply a small fraction (notably fish from St. Pierre and Miquelon and rice from French Indo-China) and the United States a considerable part (about 16 per cent of the total in 1936), including prepared foods, salt meat, flour, potatoes, lumber, and automobiles (especially Fords and Chevrolets).

TRANSPORTATION AND COMMUNICATIONS

Nearly 700 ships entered and left Guadeloupe during the year 1936, about one-half of them French. The remainder were divided among the following nationalities in order: British, Norwegian, Danish, American, and Dutch, with one or two each from Panama, Sweden, Germany, and Venezuela.

The principal harbor, Pointe-à-Pitre, is protected to the south by coral banks and islets and to the east and west by the bulk of the two main islands but is unfortunately exposed to hurricanes from the southeast. An almost straight channel 590 feet long and 30 feet deep permits ocean-going vessels to dock. This harbor and that of Fort-de-France in Martinique are the best in the central section of the Lesser Antilles.

The communication system as compared with those of some of the other West Indian islands is fairly good. There are some 252 miles of surfaced roads, 406 miles of secondary roads, and 100 miles of narrow-guage sugar railroads, but no passenger railroads. Telephone and telegraph facilities are adequate.

THE DEPENDENCIES

The Nearer Dependencies

Marie-Galante, like Grande-Terre, is a low-lying limestone island; its central plateau does not exceed 700 feet in elevation. There are practically no streams, and at times the island suffers from droughts. However, it supports 15,182 inhabitants, with a density of 270 persons to the square mile. The principal product is sugar cane, and there are three sugar factories on the island. Chief towns: Grand Bourg and Capesterre.

Désirade is also a dry limestone island with a maximum elevation of 910 feet. It produces cotton and sisal, which is used in the manufacture of twine. Fishing and grazing of sheep are also important activities. The population numbers 1558 (including Petite-Terre), and the principal town is Grande-Anse. There is a leprosorium on the island.

Les Saintes, tiny volcanic islands with a maximum elevation of about 1000 feet, are inhabited by the descendants of Breton fishermen. Most of the population of 1765 make their living from fishing, the manufacture of charcoal, and the building of boats. A small amount of sugar and coffee is grown. The climate is unusually healthful, and the islands have been called the sanatorium par excellence of the Antilles.

The limestone islets of *Petite-Terre* are of little consequence from an economic point of view.

St. Barthélemy

St. Barthélemy, a small volcanic island lying 75 miles northwest of Guadeloupe, is so dry that the inhabitants use cisterns to catch water for drinking and domestic purposes. The highest elevation is about 1000 feet. The population numbered 2519 in 1931. Gustavia, the principal town, has an excellent harbor. The island was ceded to Sweden in 1784 but was returned to France by treaty in 1877.

The principal products are cotton, pineapples, corn, manioc, cattle, and goats. Several salt-evaporating pans are operated and there is a good deal of fishing, salt fish being exported. Small deposits of lead and zinc have been mined in the past but are of no importance today. Hats, made from the fiber of a local palm, are exported.

As far as world trade is concerned, St. Barthélemy is of almost no economic value.

St. Martin

St. Martin was occupied simultaneously by the Dutch and the French in 1648, but, instead of fighting over it, the two powers divided it between them, the northern half going to France and the southern to the Netherlands. The French portion had a population of 4284 inhabitants in 1931. The highest hill rises to an elevation of 584 feet. As there are practically no flowing streams, cisterns are utilized to provide drinking water. Marigot, the capital, has a good harbor, but it has not been developed because of the dryness, small size, and limited resources of the island. A small amount of sugar and cotton and some tropical fruits and vegetables for local use are the principal products. Occupations include fishing, grazing, and the evaporation of water for salt. Limestone for building is available, and some pottery is made. Many of the people speak English, and there is a Protestant church.

FRENCH GUIANA

Government. Executive branch: Governor assisted by Privy Council of 7 members. Legislative branch: Council-General of 8 members elected by resident French citizens. Representation in French Parliament: one deputy.

Since June 6, 1930, French Guiana has been divided into two administrative sections. The area extending approximately 25 miles inland from the coast and comprising some 3700 square miles remains as the Colony of Guiana. The interior now forms the autonomous Territory of Inini (about 31,000 square miles) under the direct control of the Governor of French Guiana.

PHYSICAL FEATURES

French Guiana, the most easterly of the three Guianas, is the only French continental possession in the Americas. The colony is roughly rectangular in shape, comprising about 34,740 square miles.

French Guiana is divided into a series of roughly parallel belts or zones, generally aligned in a northwest-southeast direction. Low rocky islets (including the Iles du Salut, the infamous Ile du Diable, Ile Royale, and others) fringe the coast. In some places near the shore hills about 500 feet high improve the drainage possibilities for town sites. Inland from these low hills and from the ocean stretches a marshy area from 15 to 25 miles wide, beyond which there is a low hilly belt along the line between French Guiana proper and Inini. The unexplored and very sparsely settled interior is a low plateau extending about 125 miles inland to a range of hills approximately 1200 feet high. On the Brazilian boundary line are the 2500-foot Tumuc Humac Mountains.

The geologic structure is little known: the bedrock is granitic and most of the formations are crystalline. The lowlands are covered to a great depth with recent alluvium.

CLIMATE AND VEGETATION

The climate is probably the greatest single physical handicap. The mean annual temperature at Cayenne (sea level) is 80° F., and there is little difference in the temperatures between any two months. The year-round high temperatures, together with a relative humidity averaging about 90 per cent, make for a very enervating and monotonous climate. The average rainfall on the coast is a little more than 130 inches a year, but in the interior, especially in the higher sections, the average is even higher (in places approximately 170 inches a year). There are two rainy seasons: May through July and November through January. February and March are the dry months, when occasional droughts occur. Onshore winds bring some relief to the warm coastal districts. French Guiana is not in the hurricane track.

The natural vegetation may be divided into three general types. Along the coast and at the mouths of the rivers, mangrove thickets and a typical marsh vegetation prevail. Farther inland in the lower areas extensive savanas cover about 740,000 acres. Beyond these, on the uplands, is a tropical rain forest, which contains many valuable species of trees.

The dense forests have been a great handicap in the penetration of the interior, where the rivers are practically the only highways. More than 20 large rivers flow generally from the southern highlands northward to the coast, but they are difficult to navigate because of many falls and rapids. In the lower areas the rivers are in flood during the wet seasons and frequently shift their courses.

HISTORICAL NOTE

The early history of the colony, as well as of the two neighboring Guianas, has been one of continual struggle against climate, disease, Indians, and raiders, of internal dissension, and of wars between the Dutch, English, French, and Portuguese, during which the colony changed hands several times. The region has been French since 1814.

Cayenne was founded in 1635 on an island at the mouth of the river of that name. Probably the greatest misfortune that has befallen French Guiana was the establishment of a prison there in 1798, to which political prisoners were sent. In 1854 it was made an official penal colony. The abolition of slavery in 1848 and the discovery of gold in 1850 sounded the death knell of the early agricultural prosperity of the country.

POPULATION

When the white man arrived, the most important Indian tribes of French Guiana were the warlike Caribs, who lived on the coast, and the more sedentary agricultural Arawaks of the interior. The Caribs are now almost extinct, but the Arawaks remain.

In 1740 the total recorded population was 566 white and 4634 black persons. In 1763 12,000 persons were brought from Alsace and northern France, but after a disastrous year all but 2000 were dead, and most of those who lived returned to France. By 1775 there were 1300 free persons and 8888 slaves.

According to the 1936 census, the civil population of the Colony of Guiana was 30,906; there were 5628 convicts in the Colony; and the population of the Territory of Inini was 6099, making a total of 42,643. These figures, however, do not include several thousand uncounted prospectors, balata bleeders, Bush Negroes, and Indians. Obviously the population has grown very slowly, and at the present time it is probably decreasing. About a quarter of the people live in Cayenne, the capital (11,704 inhabitants in 1936), and most of the rest within 25 miles of the coast. The other towns, no one of which has more than 2000 inhabitants, are on rivers or at the river mouths, since there is virtually no other means of communication.

SOCIAL CONDITIONS

French Guiana has long been considered a blot on South America. All three Guianas have been among the most difficult regions of the continent to colonize, but of the three, the French colony has shown the least progress. It is also the least suitable for habitation as well as the least known.

The difficulties result from an unfortunate combination of physical, political, and social conditions. The great amount of low, swampy land, the continually high temperatures, the heavy rainfall, the dense vegetation, and tropical pests have all retarded development. Since, however, the three Guianas have similar physical conditions, the differences in social and economic status must be largely due to factors of colonial and governmental policy.

Labeled one of the worst pestholes and penal settlements in the tropics, French Guiana has suffered from a lack of favorable opinion and understanding, not only in France, but throughout the world, and inevitably there has been little interest in developing it. If money were available for the introduction of modern, wide-scale sanitation systems and adequate communication facilities, it might become an entirely different type of colony, since it is not without valuable natural resources.

In the communes there are probably 6500 male adults, almost all of whom tend to avoid sustained physical effort. The penal element includes about 1300 freed prisoners and 5500 prisoners, but age and illness exclude many of these from effective work, leaving perhaps 3000 prison laborers available. These figures show that there is a serious shortage of labor, in view of the size of the colony, the difficulty of clearing the forests for plantations, and the fact that mining and forestry, the two most important industries, both require a large labor supply. The population of Inini is made up for the most part of wandering Indians, prospectors, and descendants of freed Negro slaves, living in a primitive subsistence economy. These people are of little use as trained laborers, although the Indians are excellent guides and rivermen and are depended upon for carrying both passengers and materials in dugouts on the upper courses of the rivers. In British Guiana Hindus and in Surinam both Hindus and Javanese have been brought in as laborers, but the French have made little effort to solve the labor problem.

PRODUCTION AND TRADE

The agriculture of French Guiana is in a deplorable state. The population is not of a rural, agricultural type. Most of the people live in the small coastal towns and are engaged mainly in commerce, although the gold mines and forest exploitations attract many of the more energetic. At one time the colony had numerous plantations, but most of them have been abandoned and overgrown. Coffee, cacao, and sugar (mostly for crude rum and alcohol) are the only remaining agricultural products of commercial importance. All three of these were once exported, but now the colony produces only two-thirds of the sugar needed for local consumption. Coffee —and Guiana was the first French colony to grow coffee—must now also be imported. Sufficient rum and alcohol are produced to meet the local demand, and small quantities are exported. There is also a small surplus of cacao and of the new and most hopeful crop, bananas. Although the country has a climate suitable for the growth of almost any tropical product, of the total area of 34,740 square miles less than 13 are under cultivation.

Dismal as it may sound, this is not the worst part of the agricultural picture: French Guiana must import even the common subsistence crops in order to feed its unusually small population. One would expect such products as oils, machinery, textiles, and flour to appear on the list of imports of a small tropical country, but French Guiana also imports from neighboring countries sugar, meat, and livestock, as well as rice, manioc, corn, and poultry, all of which either have been or could be produced by the colony itself.

Great savana areas could be utilized for stock raising. While it is true that these savanas are far from ideal for cattle because of pests, floods, occasional droughts, and high temperatures, the fact remains that in 1775 16,000 head of cattle were raised in the country. This figure has steadily declined: in 1872 there were 11,000 head; in 1888, 9000; in 1912, 4600; and in 1931, only 2655. Imports of livestock come from Venezuela, where the animals are raised in much the same type of environment as that of French Guiana.

There is little doubt of the richness of the great tropical forests of French Guiana. However, the market for the forest products is not extensive, and the prices are not high enough to pay for the exploitation of the woods in remote areas. In past years the bleeding of balata for gum was important. In 1923 the exports of that commodity were 603 metric tons, valued at 14,000,000 francs. Owing to ruthless methods of exploitation, the export figure had dropped to 20 metric tons, valued at 200,000 francs, in 1932, and in 1937 the exports were valued at only 14,000 francs.

Rosewood extract, the price of which has varied from 23 to 250 francs per kilogram, is exported to France, the exports in 1937 being valued at 1,336,000 francs. Some of the rosewood is also exported. Tannin is extracted from the red mangrove but not in commercially important quantities.

Mining is the principal industry. Although there are deposits of gold, iron, copper, silver, lead, mercury, and phosphates, and possibly small amounts of platinum and diamonds, gold alone is valuable enough to pay the costs of mining and transportation. Since 1926 the exports have been stabilized at about 49,380 ounces annually. This is about half of the figure for the period between 1903 and 1917. The total amount of gold exported between 1853 and 1935 was 5,244,400 ounces. The gold is mined in placer workings in the interior, especially in the central and north-central sections of Inini. Although the gold is fairly common in the river gravels, it is difficult to find areas where the gravels are of a high enough grade to make commercial exploitation profitable. All the concessions are theoretically under the control of the colony and all exports charged with an export tax, but in the little-known and practically unpatrolled wilderness of Inini many prospectors operate illicitly.

The value of the imports of French Guiana has exceeded that of the exports in nearly every year. In 1937 the total imports amounted to 52,709,-000 francs and the exports to 36,854,000 francs. Most of the commerce is carried on with France and other French colonies. This, however, applies rather more to the imports than to the exports, because some of the gold and wood products go to various other countries.

Transportation and Communications

French Guiana has only four accessible ports: Cayenne, St. Laurent du Maroni, St. Georges du Oyapock, and Regina. Only the first two of these can handle medium-sized ships, and even at Cayenne ships cannot dock. There is practically no land communication with the neighboring countries, Surinam to the west and Brazil to the east and south. There are no railroads. Most of the principal coastal towns are connected by a road about 140 miles long from Cayenne to St. Laurent; another road runs less than 25 miles inland from the capital, and a route is projected toward the placer mines at St. Élie. Planes of the Pan American Airways land once a week at Cayenne with both passengers and mail.

CLIPPERTON ISLAND

Clipperton Island, a tiny, reef-fringed atoll 500 miles west of Costa Rica and 670 miles southwest of Acapulco on the Pacific coast of Mexico, has attracted a surprising amount of international attention.

The total land surface of 3.1 square miles consists of a circular sandy beach enclosing a lagoon about two miles in diameter with a maximum depth of several hundred feet. The beach varies from a few feet to about a quarter of a mile in width. As the maximum height of the beach is only 15 feet, waves break across the island during severe storms. On the southeastern edge of the island rises a jagged rock 62 feet high, known as Clipperton Rock, and there are five small islets in the lagoon, called "The Eggs." Some years ago there were two connections between the sea and the lagoon, but they have been filled in. The vegetation consists of a few palm trees and some low, spiny plants. At one time there were small deposits of guano, but in 1933 a French expedition failed to find any.

The island is at present uninhabited, but a few people could probably exist there by catching rain water, fishing, and gathering birds' eggs.

Reputedly discovered by Cortez in 1523, Clipperton was formally claimed for France on November 17, 1858. A party of Americans in search of guano occupied it in 1897, and France protested. When the Americans were withdrawn, a Mexican party of thirty men and women were left on the island. Apparently they were forgotten, and thirty years later only two women and a man were found alive. The dispute over the ownership of the island was submitted to the King of Italy in 1908 for arbitration, and in 1931 the decision was finally rendered in favor of France.

Clipperton cannot be used as a harbor because the outlying reefs are dangerous for ships to approach and there is no protection from storms. The central lagoon might conceivably be used by sea planes, although The Eggs would constitute a handicap. The only possible military value of Clipperton would be as a storage base for raiders of the shipping lanes between Australia and Hawaii and the Panama Canal. An emergency landing field might possibly be constructed there.

THE NETHERLANDS TERRITORIES

The Netherlands West Indies consist of two administrative "Territories" (*Gebiedsdeelen*): Curaçao, including the island of that name and five other main islands in the Lesser Antilles, and Surinam (Netherlands Guiana) on the mainland of South America.

THE TERRITORY OF CURAÇAO

Government. Executive branch: Governor, Advisory Council, consisting of the Governor as President, a Vice-President, and three other members, all appointed by the crown. Legislative branch: "States" (legislative assembly), consisting of 15 members, of whom 5 are appointed by the crown upon recommendation of the Advisory Council and 10 are elected.

Suffrage is limited to males and restricted by income or educational qualifications. In 1937 the electorate numbered 2754 out of a total population of 94,945.

AREA AND PHYSICAL FEATURES

The Territory has a total area of some 384 square miles,[1] or about a quarter that of Rhode Island. The islands form two groups lying at almost opposite ends of the curving chain of the Lesser Antilles. The southern group ("Benedenwindsche Eilanden"), 20 to 60 miles off the Venezuelan coast, comprises the islands of Aruba (70 sq. mi.), Curaçao (170 sq. mi.), and Bonaire (108 sq. mi.). The northern group ("Bovenwindsche Eilanden"), some 500 miles to the northeast, comprises St. Eustatius ("Statia," 12 sq. mi.), Saba (5 sq. mi.), and the southern part of St. Martin (St. Maarten, 13 sq. mi.), the northern part being French.

Saba and St. Eustatius belong to the main chain of volcanic islands of the Lesser Antilles. They are built of relatively young volcanic materials: lavas, loose ash, stones, and boulders. A well preserved extinct cone (1975 ft.) with a crater occupies the southern part of St. Eustatius, and a more thoroughly dissected cone (965 ft.) the northern part. Saba is a single dissected cone rising to a height of 2887 feet. St. Martin, on the other hand, is one of the outer fringe of islands bordering the volcanic chain from Guadeloupe northward (see p. 17) in which there are no recent volcanic forms. In the French part of St. Martin a foundation of old volcanic rocks has been partly overlaid with calcareous deposits, but in the Dutch part volcanic rocks (quartz-diorites) predominate. The highest point is on the boundary in the interior (1266 ft.).

In the southern islands there has been no volcanic activity in recent geological times. All three islands are lower than those of the northern group (highest point on Curaçao, 1220 ft.; on Aruba, 617 ft.; on Bonaire, 787 ft.). Upon the relatively level surface of much-worn-down volcanic rocks and remnants of sedimentary rocks limestones were laid down at a

---

[1] The figures for areas are from the booklet "Curaçao," published by K. Vereeniging "Oost en West," The Hague, 4th ed., 1939. The total includes Little Curaçao and Little Bonaire, which together have an area of about 6 square miles.

time when the surface was submerged beneath the sea. The present islands owe their origin to subsequent uparchings of the limestones and their foundation rocks along lines that trend about northwest-southeast.

On Curaçao and Aruba erosion has removed most, and on Bonaire a part, of the limestone, exposing the underlying predominantly volcanic basement rocks, which erode more easily. The limestone, however, has not been entirely stripped away from Curaçao and Aruba, but some of the original cover remains in the form of discontinuous ridges or cuestas around the coasts. A slight recent lowering of the land in relation to sea level has permitted the sea to "drown" certain of the steep-walled valleys that cut through these coastal ridges as well as part of the wider valleys behind the limestone ridges. This is the origin of the distinctive fan-

TABLE V: CURAÇAO AND ST. MARTIN: TEMPERATURE DATA
(Degrees F.)

Temperature	Curaçao (1910–1933)	Philipsburg, St. Martin (1920–1933)
Mean annual	81.0	79.7
Mean, warmest month	83.3 (Sept.)	82.2 (Aug., Sept.)
Mean, coolest month	78.4 (Jan.)	76.5 (Jan., Feb.)

shaped embayments with their bottle-neck entrances that are found on Curaçao and Bonaire—for example, the harbor of Willemstad on Curaçao consists of St. Anna Bay, a narrow passageway through the limestone, leading into the extensive basin of the Schottegat.

Exposed to surf driven by the prevailing northeasterly trade winds, the windward coasts of Aruba and Curaçao are cliff-lined and almost harborless. A coral barrier reef fringes the leeward side of Aruba, separated from the shore by lagoons, but on Curaçao the coral reefs along the leeward side are attached to the mainland.

Over the southern and most of the central part of Bonaire limestones of recent origin form a low and generally level surface, but in the central and northern parts of the island erosion has sculptured the older, and for the most part volcanic, rocks to form a hilly terrain.

CLIMATE

The islands lie in the zone of the trade winds, which blow with great steadiness from the east and northeast. Normally the variation in temperature between the seasons is less marked than that between day and night. The evenness of the temperature is evident from Table V.

All the islands receive a somewhat scanty rainfall, but those of the northern group are the more fortunate, in that the precipitation is not only about twice as great as in the southern islands but is more dependable. Nowhere, however, is the rainfall sufficient to maintain continuously flowing streams. Rainfall figures for Curaçao and St. Martin are shown in Table VI.

In the three southern islands, which may be said to have a tropical steppe climate, the problem of drought is perennially serious. Wells are maintained by the government in the country districts. Two plants are operated on Curaçao and one on Aruba for distilling sea water for use when other sources give out. In the northern islands there are some wells

TABLE VI: WILLEMSTAD AND ST. MARTIN: PRECIPITATION DATA
(Inches)

Rainfall	Willemstad (1894–1933)	Philipsburg, St. Martin (1892–1933)
Mean annual	22.0	42.6
Mean, rainiest month	5.0 (Nov.)	5.8 (Nov.)
Mean, driest month	0.5 (May)	1.6 (Mar.)

(only three on Saba), but most of the drinking water is collected in cisterns.

The northern islands lie in the path of the hurricanes, but the southern group is somewhat to the south of the main path.

NATURAL VEGETATION

The natural vegetation of the southern islands reflects the dry climate. Drought-resistant plants, such as cacti, agaves, and aloes, predominate. Along the exposed, wind-swept northeastern coasts there are barren tracts, and the low-lying shores of the lagoons are fringed with mangroves. In the wetter northern islands the natural vegetation is more luxuriant: at the lower levels, however, much of it is a drought-resistant bush. Low evergreen trees and shrubs are found at higher altitudes, and there are scattered patches of tropical rain forest at the highest elevations on Saba and St. Eustatius. Throughout the Territory man has greatly altered the original vegetation by grazing, particularly of goats, and by cutting.

HISTORICAL NOTE

Discovered by Amerigo Vespucci in 1499 and first occupied by the Spanish in 1527, Curaçao was almost forgotten until the Dutch drove out the Spanish in 1634 and established a settlement there. Aruba and Bonaire were also occupied by the Dutch at about the same time. In 1643 Peter Stuyvesant was sent to Curaçao as governor, and under his regime the colony was developed into a great commercial center for the whole Caribbean region—a center whose prosperity was largely dependent on the slave trade. The British captured and held Curaçao during the Napoleonic period, but, along with the other islands of the present Territory, it was restored to the Dutch in 1814 and has remained in their hands ever since. The decline of the slave trade and its final abolition early in the nineteenth century ended the prosperity of the islands for a time, but it was again restored by the establishment of the oil industry on Curaçao in 1916 and on Aruba in 1925.

The Dutch occupied St. Eustatius in 1635 and Saba in 1640. The French and the Dutch established themselves on St. Martin in 1638 only to be

TABLE VII: TERRITORY OF CURAÇAO: POPULATION DATA

Island	1870	1915	1938
Curaçao	20,844	33,677	62,798
Aruba	3,792	9,204	28,155
Bonaire	3,816	6,592	5,536
St. Martin	2,853	3,202	2,202
St. Eustatius	1,890	1,431	1,121
Saba	1,832	2,488	1,209

driven out by the Spanish in 1640. The island was recovered by the French and the Dutch in 1648 and divided peaceably between them. In the eighteenth century St. Eustatius became an important trading center. "Sometimes as many as seven hundred ships lay in the Statia roads at one time." During the American revolution St. Eustatius was one of the most important points from which supplies were shipped to the American colonies, but when the British captured it in 1781 a blow was dealt to its prosperity from which the island has never recovered. In its more fortunate days "Statia" had many prosperous estates, on which sugar cane, tobacco, and other crops were raised, but today there is little cultivation there, and the population is dwindling, as in the other islands of the northern group.

POPULATION

The total population of the Territory increased from 35,027 in 1870 to 101,021 in 1938, an increase due entirely to gains on Curaçao, Aruba, and to a lesser degree on Bonaire, for the three northern islands suffered a net loss (from 6575 in 1870 to 4532 in 1938). In both 1870 and 1938 about 60 per cent of all the people resided on Curaçao, most of them in the commercial and industrial center of Willemstad and its environs. In 1938 Curaçao had twice, and Aruba three times, as many people as in 1915, the gains having been due primarily to the establishment of the oil refineries. The population of Bonaire reached a peak of 8888 people in 1921, but thereafter declined to 5536 in 1938, mainly because of the migration of workers to Aruba and Curaçao (see Table VII).

In 1937 the birth rate for the Territory was 32.2 per 1000 and the death rate 10.84 per 1000.

No census data are available on the racial composition of the population, but Negroes and mulattoes constitute by far the largest group, perhaps between 80 and 90 per cent of the total. In the three northern islands, especially in Saba, the proportion of whites is somewhat larger than in the

TABLE VIII: TERRITORY OF CURAÇAO: IMPORTS AND EXPORTS, 1933–1938
(Values in thousands of guilders)

	1933	1934	1935	1936	1937	1938
Imports	150,269	154,822	174,165	197,012	297,286	391,130
Exports	194,560	161,350	167,257	210,513	269,944	340,545

southern islands, and English is the principal language. In the southern islands the older Negro and white populations speak a curious dialect known as Papiamento, derived mainly from Spanish (or from Portuguese, according to one authority) with a mingling of Dutch, Portuguese, English, and Carib elements. During and since the World War and especially since about 1930 colored immigrants have come to Curaçao and Aruba in large numbers from other parts of the Caribbean region to work in the refineries and on the water front. They have been joined by Syrians, Hindus, Chinese, Portuguese from the Azores and Madeira, and whites from the Netherlands, England, the United States, Venezuela, Colombia, etc. The population of these two islands has thus become quite cosmopolitan.

PRODUCTION AND TRADE

The exports and imports of the Territory increased progressively from 1933 through 1938, the latest year for which the figures are available (see Table VIII). Table IX shows the supreme importance of petroleum in the commerce of the islands. Oil refineries were established by Dutch and English interests on Curaçao at the time of the World War, and the refinery at Emmastad on the Schottegat near Willemstad is said to be one of the largest in the world. In 1925 Dutch-English and American oil companies built refineries on Aruba, which now exceed those of Curaçao in the export value of their products. Of the total imports of crude oil $(226,650^2)$ by far the greater part comes from Venezuela, especially from the oil fields in the vicinity of Lake Maracaibo, although some is imported from the eastern Venezuelan fields, from Colombia, and from Trinidad. Owing to shallow water at the mouth of Lake Maracaibo, large ships cannot enter, and hence the oil must be transported to Curaçao and Aruba in light-draft vessels. Good harbors, proximity to the Venezuelan fields, and a stable government combined to attract the industry to these islands.

2 All figures for values in this section (pp. 74–78) are in thousands of guilders and are for 1937 except where otherwise indicated.

That the oil industry has been rapidly expanding is indicated both by the recent increase in population on the two islands and by the fact that between 1933 and 1937 the value of the imports of petroleum and its products rose from 129,032 to 254,174 and that of the exports rose from 166,131 in 1935 to 266,667 in 1937. (The figures for the total trade of the Territory, Table VIII, show that there was a further notable rise in 1938.)

TABLE IX: TERRITORY OF CURAÇAO: IMPORTS AND EXPORTS, 1937
(Values in thousands of guilders)

Imports	Total		From the U.S.A.	From other points in W. Hemi-sphere	From other parts of the world
	Value	%	Value	Value	Value
Petroleum and Products	254,174	85.5	16,747	237,244	183
Foods and Beverages	7,058	2.4	2,952	1,384	2,722
All other Products	36,054	12.1	17,933	1,696	16,425
Total	297,286	100.0	37,632	240,324	19,330

Exports	Total		To the U.S.A.	To other points in W. Hemi-sphere	To other parts of the world
	Value	%	Value	Value	Value
Petroleum and Products	266,667	98.8	31,946	38,594	196,127
Food and Beverages	144	0.1	1	28	115
All other Products	3,133	1.1	625	26	2,482
Total	269,944	100.0	32,572	38,648	198,724

In 1937 the value of oil imports to Aruba amounted to 141,477 and of exports from Aruba to 149,303, the corresponding figures for Curaçao being 112,690 and 117,364. Most of the petroleum exports go to Europe, especially to England (33.1 per cent in 1937); the Netherlands' share was about 8 per cent; and that of the United States about 12.

The principal petroleum products exported are gasoline (value for

Aruba, 62,437; Curaçao, 28,921), fuel oil (Aruba, 55,518; Curaçao, 52,394), gas oil (Aruba, 9019; Curaçao 16,359), and Diesel oil (Aruba, 14,675; Curaçao, 6300). In 1937 about two-thirds of the gasoline exported from each island (value for Aruba, 38,575; Curaçao, 18,705), one-fifth of the fuel oil from Curaçao (10,693), and one-ninth of the fuel oil from Aruba (6712) went to England. Nearly half of the fuel oil exported from Aruba (23,065) went to the United States.

Table IX shows that only about 14.5 per cent of the total imports into the Territory in 1937 and less than 1.2 per cent of the total exports were of commodities other than petroleum and its products. The value of the

TABLE X: TERRITORY OF CURAÇAO: IMPORTS AND EXPORTS OF NON-PETROLEUM PRODUCTS BY ISLANDS, 1937
(Values in thousands of guilders)

Curaçao	Imports	Exports
Curaçao	25,504	2,438
Aruba	17,252	774
Bonaire	136	50
St. Martin	118	9
St. Eustatius	45	5
Saba	57	0.5

non-petroleum imports so greatly exceeded that of the non-petroleum exports that the balance of trade as a whole was unfavorable, despite the fact that petroleum exports exceeded petroleum imports in value. The relative commercial importance of the six islands in their trade in non-petroleum products is suggested by Table X.

The principal product derived from the natural resources of the Territory is phosphate of lime obtained from ancient transformed guano deposits. This was formerly mined both on Aruba and Curaçao but is now exploited only on the latter (value, 873). It is exported almost entirely to Finland, Denmark, Germany, and the Netherlands. Salt for export is produced from salinas on the shores of Bonaire (value, 4.2) and St. Martin (6.6).

The manufacture of straw hats for export to the United States has long been a household industry on Curaçao Island (value, 92.9). The hats are made from the leaves of a palmetto (*Carludovica palmata*), imported mainly from the Maracaibo region of Venezuela.

The northern islands are too small and the southern islands too dry for agricultural production of any consequence, and even in the northern islands the somewhat scanty and poorly distributed rainfall limits the productivity of the inherently fertile volcanic soils.

About 60 per cent of the total land area of Curaçao and 56 per cent of that of Bonaire is in the hands of large proprietors—owners of more than

100 hectares (247 acres) each—the remainder belonging to small proprietors and to the government. On Aruba, however, only 2.5 per cent
belongs to large proprietors, and nearly all the rest is government-owned.
Small land holdings prevail in the northern islands. The large holdings are
no longer prosperous, owing to high costs of labor, decreasing prices,
competition, and increasingly heavy tax burdens. Since the population can
find employment in industry, much land that was formerly cultivated both
in large and small holdings has been abandoned or given over to livestock.

Table XI shows clearly the importance of goat and sheep raising in the
economy of the islands. Goatskins valued at 207 thousand guilders were

TABLE XI: TERRITORY OF CURAÇAO: NUMBER OF LIVESTOCK
BY ISLANDS, 1937

Island	Goats	Sheep	Cattle	Asses	Pigs	Horses	Mules
Curaçao	23,401	7,628	1,604	2,231	1,626	56	21
Aruba	11,080	14,150	915	845	1,023	5	..
Bonaire	*30,000	*11,000	20	1,000	440	52	2
St. Martin	1,196	1,157	1,249	88	335	63	..
St. Eustatius	887	1,286	815	417	321	41	1
Saba	529	274	162	60	209	12	..
Total	*67,000	*35,000	4,765	4,641	3,954	229	24

*Round numbers

exported in 1937, a value greater than that of any other locally derived
product with the exception of phosphates. Between 1932 and 1937 the
number of goats and of cattle showed a net increase in every island, the
increase in goats being especially marked on Bonaire, Aruba, and St.
Martin, and that in cattle on Curaçao, Aruba, and St. Martin. Sheep also
increased in number on all the islands but Curaçao and St. Martin; on
Bonaire the number rose from 3500 in 1932 to 11,000 in 1937. Notable
also are the relatively large number of cattle on the northern islands,
their almost complete absence on Bonaire, and the limited use of horses
and mules as compared with that of asses.

Sorghum is the principal subsistence crop. On Curaçao and Aruba
truck gardens, many of them cultivated by Chinese, supply the local market,
and fruits (mangroves, guavas, papayas, watermelons, coconuts, oranges,
lemons) are raised for local consumption in hofjes or patches of irrigated
garden land on certain of the farms. Aloes are cultivated on Aruba and
Bonaire and exported (value, 111) to the United States, and divi-divi
pods, for use in tanning, were exported from Curaçao and Bonaire to
Germany and the Netherlands (32.4). A very small quantity of orange
peel was exported to Germany and the Netherlands for use in the manu-

facture of Curaçao liqueur (2.5), and eight small establishments were
engaged in making this liqueur for local consumption. St. Eustatius exports sweet potatoes and yams in small quantities (3.1). On St. Martin
and St. Eustatius most of the land is given over to the pasturing of cattle,
sheep, and goats. Except for steep hillside gardens, there is little or no
agriculture in Saba: the men are sailors, the women make some lace.

The value of all non-petroleum imports for the Territory increased
from 21,237 in 1933 to 43,112 in 1937. By countries, the percentages of
these in 1933 were: U. S. A., 44; Netherlands, 16; England, 6.3; Venezuela,
4.4; Japan, 3.7; and in 1937, U. S. A., 48.4; Netherlands, 21; Japan, 6.8;
Germany 6.0; England, 5.4. Of the imports of non-petroleum products
the bulk comes to Curaçao and Aruba and consists of machinery, iron
and steel, tubes, pipes, and other materials used in the oil industry[3] and of
building materials, textiles and other manufactures, and food stuffs (especially sterilized milk, butter, meat, eggs, and flour) for the population.
The imports to Bonaire and the three northern islands are primarily flour
and other food products, textiles and other manufactured goods, and
timber.

After 1937 there was a notable increase in the trade of the Territory
with the United States and the Netherlands, especially in imports from
these countries. Imports from the United States jumped in value from
37,632 in 1937 to 82,514 in 1938, but declined to 62,487 in 1939; from
the Netherlands they increased from 8878 in 1937 to 17,670 in 1938 and
to 18,897 in 1939. Exports to the United States in the three successive
years were 32,572, 41,546, and 37,759, and to the Netherlands 27,504,
38,433, and 26,066. These figures, it should be noted, are for the total
trade, including petroleum and its products.

The prosperity attending the development of the oil industry is reflected
in governmental revenues now normally in excess of expenditures. Prior
to 1924 and again in 1928–1931, however, the home government of the
Netherlands was obliged to make an annual contribution toward the ex-
penses of administration and governmental services.

TRANSPORTATION

Willemstad on Curaçao has one of the finest and most advantageously
situated harbors in the West Indies.[4] Seldom visited by hurricanes, it lies
not far from the shortest routes from Europe to the west coast of South
America by way of the Panama Canal and directly on the routes from
the Pacific and Gulf coasts of the United States to Venezuela, the Guianas,
and Brazil. Thus long before the rise of the oil industry it had served as
an entrepôt and coal-fueling station. It is one of the largest warehousing
centers in the Caribbean and one of the busiest points of transshipment

3 For Curaçao these were valued at 9700 in 1937 and 16,158 in 1938, or about 38 and
39 per cent respectively of the total value of non-petroleum imports into that island.
4 On harbors, airports, and seaplane bases see pp. 94 and 95.

for passengers and merchandise carried by ship and by plane. Moreover, "in a certain sense it is not an entrepôt but a regular sea port serving the Maracaibo Basin in much the same way that a river mouth may serve its valley."[5]

In normal times the islands have been interconnected by mail steamers running three times a week each way between Curaçao and Aruba and every two weeks between Curaçao and the northern islands, stopping at Bonaire. Planes run frequently between Curaçao and Aruba. Travel between the islands of the northern group is ordinarily by sailing vessel only.

There are good black-surfaced roads on the southern islands, especially Curaçao and Aruba. Automobiles are used on these islands as well as on Bonaire and St. Martin. On Saba and St. Eustatius transportation is mainly by horse or donkey.

SURINAM (NETHERLANDS GUIANA)

Government. The governmental machinery of Surinam is similar to that of Curaçao. The Governor and Council are appointed by the crown. The States consist of 15 members, 10 elected by the citizens according to an elective system based on educational or income qualifications and 5 appointed by the Governor. The budget must be approved by the States-General in the Netherlands, since governmental expenditures exceed revenues and have to be made good by annual subsidies from the home treasury (see below, p. 85).

PHYSICAL FEATURES

Surinam has an area of about 50,000 square miles, or approximately that of Wisconsin. The Territory may be divided into three main zones roughly parallel with the coast: a narrow, alluvial coastal plain 10 to 50 miles wide, a belt of "savanas" about 30 to 40 miles wide, and the little-known hilly to mountainous region in the interior, which comprises most of the country.

The low shifting shore line is fringed by mud banks, and ships can approach only through the estuaries. Part of the salt marshland was diked, drained, and converted into polders by Dutch planters with slave labor in the eighteenth and early nineteenth centuries. The heavy marine clays of the coastal strip are very fertile and are indeed the only part of the Territory in which cultivation is practicable under present conditions.

The "savana" zone is somewhat hilly; a sparse forest is here interrupted by open areas on which only shrubs grow. There are desolate sandy areas and some swamps. Most of the zone is worthless for agricultural purposes. Strips of alluvial soil along the rivers, however, offer local areas suitable for small farms but not for large-scale commercial plantations.

The interior is inhabited only by a few Indians and Bush Negroes. The general level is between 300 and 1600 feet, although the summits of the

---

[5]R. S. Platt: A Curaçao Farmstead, *Journ. of Geogr.*, Vol. 35, 1936, pp. 154–156; reference on p. 154.

Wilhelmina Mountains near the center of the Territory, rise above 3000 feet (highest peak 4120 feet). Most of the interior is covered with virgin tropical rain forest, though there is an area of true grassy savana near the Brazilian border. Logging and balata bleeding are the principal industries. Access to the interior is almost exclusively by river and is difficult owing to many falls and rapids.

CLIMATE

The climate is everywhere tropical, characterized by high temperatures with small seasonal variations. Along the coast the steady trade winds from the east-northeast and east moderate the extremes of temperature. There are two rainy and two dry seasons. The driest part of the territory is the western coastal area, and the rainiest is in the interior. Severe droughts occur occasionally. Surinam lies entirely outside the hurricane zone.

TABLE XII—PARAMARIBO: TEMPERATURE AND PRECIPITATION DATA

Mean temperature 1899–1933	Degrees F.	Mean precipitation 1847–1933	Inches
Annual	79.0	Annual	91.0
Warmest month	80.9 (Sept.)	Rainiest month	12.2 (May)
Coolest month	77.5 (January)	Driest month	3.0 (October)

HISTORICAL NOTE

Dutch traders began to visit the Guiana coast before 1600, Dutch settlements were founded in what is now British Guiana in 1621, and the Dutch held that region until nearly the end of the eighteenth century. The first settlements in Surinam, however, were made by the British, near the present site of Paramaribo in 1630. During the following thirty years the colony was established on an agricultural basis by Francis Willoughby, governor of Barbados, and sugar plantations were developed. Refugees from Holland, Italy, and Brazil, including many Jews, were encouraged to settle in the region. During the Anglo-Dutch War of 1665–1667 Surinam was seized by the Dutch, who retained it by the Treaty of Breda, 1667 (the treaty which confirmed English possession of New Amsterdam). Cacao was introduced in 1685, coffee (from Java) about 1700, and cotton in 1752. The colony was twice held by the British (1799–1802, 1804–1814) during the Napoleonic period but was finally restored to the Dutch in 1815. Sugar production declined in the nineteenth century, and cotton growing had practically disappeared by the end of the century. Following the abolition of slavery in 1863, an agreement was made with Great Britain in 1870 to permit the immigration of contract laborers from India.

POPULATION AND SOCIAL CONDITIONS

The population of Surinam, now about 178,000 (177,980, December 31,

1939), has more than doubled in the last fifty years. It is made up of the following elements in the approximate numbers indicated: Negroes and half-breeds, 66,000; British Indians, 42,000; Javanese, 34,000; Bush Negroes, 17,000; aboriginal Indians, 3500; Chinese, 2200; Dutch, 1000; other Europeans, 1000. The death rate for Surinam during recent years has averaged about 12 and the birth rate about 31 per 1000.

The population of Paramaribo, the capital, was 28,831 in 1890 and 54,852 in 1939. This rapid growth has taxed the housing accommodations. In 1939 about 11,000 persons in Paramaribo lived in houses of one room, and 12,000 in houses of two rooms. The average number of occupants of the one-room houses was three and of the two-room houses four. The second largest town, Nieuw Nickerie, has about 4000 inhabitants.

The greater part of the population is engaged in farming. The abolition of slavery in 1863 was a severe blow to the planters, whose prosperity had been based on slave labor, and was followed by the abandonment of many estates. In order to obtain a more dependable labor supply than that provided by the former slave population, immigration of Orientals was encouraged until 1931. Between 1873 and 1916, when the practice was discontinued, 34,024 British Indians were imported as contract laborers, and 32,020 Javanese were brought in between 1853 and 1931. The large plantations are today worked mainly by these two groups. It is said that the British Indians are hard workers but tend to be somewhat undependable and troublesome. The Javanese, though less efficient, spend their wages freely and stick to their jobs. Many small holdings are now in the hands of the Indians and Javanese. In recent years three shipments of Javanese have entered as free immigrants to establish themselves as small farmers on government settlement projects. The Bush Negroes, descendants of runaway slaves who took to the interior, live in small groups, raise a few subsistence crops such as rice, and further support themselves, as do the Indians, by hunting and fishing.

The small farmers, who with their families comprise 70 per cent of the population, used to supplement their income by part-time work on the large plantations. Since the outbreak of the present war, however, they have been in considerable difficulty. With the closing of the normal export markets for coffee and sugar, the plantations have hardly been able to find work for their formerly full-time laborers, a good many of whom have migrated to Paramaribo, where the problem of unemployment has become serious. The government is attempting to deal with this problem by providing full and part-time employment on the roads and by placing unemployed plantation and town workers upon small holdings in the country.

The war has brought about a pronounced increase in the cost of living. Between September 15, 1936, and August 15, 1940, the indexes of the costs of imported foodstuffs and clothing rose 38.1 and 69.8 per cent, respectively, and that of local products rose 12.5 per cent.

PRODUCTION

The total cultivated area in the Territory is estimated at some 150 square miles, of which about one-third is in large plantations and the rest in small peasant holdings. The cultivated land is confined almost exclusively to the clay belt along the coast, where the small-scale farms are very much scattered and the small farmers have a difficult struggle with the water. A recent investigation has shown that about 1400 square miles of the clay belt has free drainage at low tide and could presumably be developed for cultivation, though with considerable initial expense.

Under slavery it was profitable to operate small plantations, but these have been largely abandoned or combined into large estates better adapted to modern methods of commercial agriculture and to the existing labor supply. In 1936 there were 51 large estates, employing 9069 laborers. Forty-eight of these, with an average of about 400 acres of cultivated land in each and employing a total of 5475 laborers, were devoted primarily to coffee. The other three, employing 3594 laborers, specialized in the production of sugar and molasses. The total acreage under cultivation on the three sugar plantations was 7571 acres of which 5854 acres were on a single estate, employing 2733 laborers.

The twelve principal crops in the order of their value in 1937 (values in thousands of guilders) were: sugar (1178), rice (1061), coffee (469), plantains (329), peanuts (212), coconuts (162), tubers (89), corn (72), cacao (49), bananas (43), vegetables (22), oranges (21). Sugar is produced exclusively and coffee largely on the estates. Except for about a third of the oranges, the other crops are raised almost wholly on small holdings.

Agricultural production in Surinam has undergone many changes and difficulties. Recently sugar, coffee, and rice have been the most important agricultural exports. In 1870 there were about 75 sugar plantations, with some 13,300 acres under cultivation and a production of 11,020 long tons. At present the three sugar plantations, with a smaller acreage under cultivation than in 1870, produce a larger quantity of sugar—15,700 tons in 1936. Surinam's sugar industry, however, is relatively of much less importance than it used to be in comparison with that of Cuba, Java, and other major sugar-producing regions. Since the failure of the banana crop in 1911, Liberian coffee has been planted much more extensively than previously. Before 1936 a considerable part of the crop was exported to the United States, but since then the American market for Liberian coffee has been virtually closed through a ruling of the New York Coffee and Sugar Exchange, and production in Surinam has been reduced as a result. Rice, cultivated primarily for domestic consumption, constitutes the largest crop in terms of quantity and the second largest in value. In 1938 20 per cent of the rice was exported, but since July 1940 its export has been legally forbidden in order to conserve the local food supply. Panama disease had virtually put an end to the raising of bananas by 1911, but there has been a slight revival since 1930. Cacao, formerly an important crop, is now raised almost wholly for local consumption. Wood and balata are obtained from the forests of the interior. Balata is the latex of the bully tree, from which is manufactured a substitute for gutta percha used in golf balls.

The principal product of the Territory is bauxite, which has been exported since 1922. A subsidiary of the Aluminum Company of America is engaged in the industry at Moengo on the Cottica River, 104 miles from its mouth, and is developing a new mine and refining plant at Paranam on the Surinam River about twenty miles above Paramaribo. Exports of bauxite increased from approximately 172,000 long tons in 1927 to 500,000 in 1939. The importance of Surinam's bauxite to the United States is evident from the following figures for 1938. Domestic production in the United States was 323,818 long tons: imports to the United States were 455,693 of which 386,756 came from Surinam and 60,044 from British

TABLE XIII—SURINAM: EXPORTS, 1937 AND 1939
(Values in thousands of guilders)

Article	Total Value	Destination Principal Countries	Share	1939 Total Value
		1937		
Bauxite	4,904	U. S. A.	All	5,294
Gold	744	Netherlands	All	607
Sugar products	682			454
Sugar		Netherlands	623	410
Rum		Netherlands and Great Britain	28	18
Molasses		British Guiana	32	25
Coffee	529	Netherlands	300	593
		Norway	164	
Rice	414	Guadeloupe Martinique French Guiana		381
Balata	190	Great Britain Norway Germany British Guiana		437
Wood	69	Various		91
Fruits	9			15
Oranges		Netherlands, Curaçao	7.3	
Bananas		Netherlands	0.8	

Guiana. Gold is also mined and, next to bauxite, is the most valuable export of the territory.

TRADE

The balance of trade of the Territory has normally been unfavorable in recent years, but in 1937 and, by a smaller margin in 1939, the increase in bauxite exports to the United States changed it to a favorable balance. In 1933 total exports were valued (in thousands of guilders) at 3802, of which 43 per cent went to the Netherlands and 38 per cent to the United States. In 1937 the value had risen to 7570, of which 25.6 per cent went to the Netherlands and 65.6 per cent to the United States. There was a falling off in the total value of exports in 1938 due almost entirely to a drop in the price of bauxite. In 1939, however, with the price of bauxite rising and shipments being made on a much larger scale, the total value of

TABLE XIV—SURINAM: IMPORTS, 1937
(Values in thousands of guilders)

Classification	Total Value	Origin of Imports Principal Countries	Share
Manufactures	3,774	Netherlands	1,260
		U. S. A.	785
		Japan	597
		Great Britain	442
		Germany	234
Food and Beverages	2,131	Netherlands	1,063
		U. S. A.	497
		Great Britain	164
		Argentina	147
Raw and partly manu-factured goods	692	U. S. A.	259
		Trinidad	172
		Netherlands	161

exports reached 7959, of which 16.5 per cent went to the Netherlands and 71.8 per cent to the United States. If the exports of bauxite (all of which were destined for the United States) were not included in the total, the proportions would have been 49 per cent to the Netherlands and 19 per cent to the United States.

Between 1933 and 1939 total imports increased in value from 4899 to 7882 (in thousands of guilders); in 1933 the Netherlands sent about 39 per cent and the United States about 20 per cent, but in 1939 the Netherlands' share had fallen to 34 per cent and that of the United States had risen to 30 per cent. There has been a steady diminution in the relative value of imports from the United Kingdom (12.3 per cent of the total in 1935 and 5.3 per cent in 1939), a slight increase in those from Japan (8.4

per cent in 1935 and 9.4 per cent in 1939), while those from Germany and Trinidad have each remained fairly constant at a little less than five per cent of the total.

Tables XIII and XIV bring out certain facts of interest in regard to the character of the foreign trade in 1937 and 1939.

Imports from the Netherlands and Great Britain consist of a great variety of manufactured articles and foodstuffs; those from the United States of meat, flour, oil, coal, and miscellaneous manufactures, among which machinery for bauxite mining operations has been an important item. Imports from Japan consist almost entirely of cotton and silk textiles and from Argentina, of beef.

The value of Surinam to the Netherlands is perhaps more moral than material. The Territory has been a liability in so far as costs of government are concerned. Since 1934 annual subsidies of 2422 to 2988 thousand guilders have been required to make good the difference between revenues and expenditures (in thousands of guilders, revenues in 1939 were 4553; expenditures, 7145; subsidy, 2592). In 1940 the deficiency was expected to be even greater. It was estimated that expenditures would amount to 7517 thousand guilders as against revenues of 4189, requiring a state subvention of 3328.

TRANSPORTATION AND HARBORS

In the more densely settled areas near the coast there are fairly good roads, and a railway leads 173 kilometers from Paramaribo to Dam on the Surinam River. A private company also operates small steamers and motor boats on the rivers. Traffic in the interior is almost exclusively by river.

Paramaribo lies 13 miles above the mouth of the Surinam River. Its one mile of developed water frontage may be reached by ships of 19-foot draft.

STRATEGIC IMPORTANCE OF THE EUROPEAN POSSESSIONS IN THE CARIBBEAN AREA

In terms of their possible strategic importance the European possessions in the Caribbean area may be considered from two points of view: (1) as sources of war materials and (2) as bases for offensive and defensive operations. Only from the first point of view would it seem that these possessions are of any strategic value to the possessor nations in the present European war. None of them command approaches to more important possessions of the same nations, as do, for example, Gibraltar, Egypt, Dakar, and Singapore. Should France declare war on Great Britain, it is conceivable, though highly improbable, that she might attempt to use her island possessions and French Guiana as naval and air bases from which to attack British shipping out of the Caribbean area, as, for example, tankers carrying oil from Trinidad and the refineries on the Dutch islands of Curaçao and Aruba.

IMPORTANCE AS SOURCES OF WAR MATERIALS

As sources of war materials only British Guiana, Surinam (Netherlands Guiana), and the islands of Trinidad, Curaçao, and Aruba are of any importance to the present possessors and to the United States or would be to an invader; the first two for their bauxite, Trinidad for its oil fields and refineries, and Curaçao and Aruba for their oil refineries and stocks of oil. The mining of manganese, recently discovered in British Guiana and believed to occur in large quantities, has not yet been undertaken on any large scale, and consequently no ore would be immediately available.

For the United States the only needed war material to be obtained from the European possessions in the Caribbean area is bauxite; and how important this is to the United States is to be judged from the fact that about 98 per cent of the country's imports of this ore now comes from British and Netherlands Guiana. Oil from Trinidad and from the refineries on Curaçao and Aruba, although not to be classed as a necessity, would be of value in conserving the country's own reserves.

To an invader, as to the present possessor nations, the bauxite mines of British and Netherlands Guiana and the oil fields of Trinidad would furnish important war materials. However, now that the axis powers have virtual control of the French and Hungarian bauxite deposits (two of the most important in the world), seizure of the Guiana deposits would be of value chiefly because it would cut off their opponents from this source. The stocks of oil at the refineries on Curaçao and Aruba, if not destroyed before they fell into the hands of the invader, would be of value as long as they lasted for fueling ships and planes; but to make these islands of any continuous importance as suppliers of oil, the invader would have to gain control also of at least the oil fields of the Maracaibo Basin in Venezuela, which now feed the refineries, and of the 250 miles of sea between the fields and the refineries. Moreover, all equipment replacements and practically all food supplies for the natives and operating personnel would have to be imported. In Curaçao and Aruba the operating and maintenance crews that would have to be brought in and the native labor that would probably be impressed into service could not live on existing stocks of food and locally grown products for more than a very short time, and even in Trinidad and the Guianas it is doubtful if they could do so.

Importance as Bases for Offensive Operations

Indeed, no sizable invading force could long live on local food supplies on any of the European possessions in the Caribbean area, and hence the ability of the axis powers to use these possessions as bases for naval and air offensive operations against the continent would depend in the first instance on their ability to control the sea routes from Europe. In time, reorganization of the local agricultural economy and substitution of the cultivation of food crops for the present specialization in a few crops for export might make it possible for most of the islands and mainland territories to supply a large part of the food requirements of the natives and of the necessary construction, maintenance, operating, and fighting crews; but it seems scarcely likely that an invader would risk the possibility of a long siege in any of the present European possessions in case the initial drive should fail. Except for timber, none of the possessions could supply materials for the construction of port facilities, landing fields, and defense works, and, except in Jamaica, Trinidad, and the Guianas, where a considerable business in lumber export is carried on, even lumber-milling equipment would have to be imported.

The Bahama Islands

The many intricate channels of the Bahama Islands were used by pirates and buccaneers in colonial times as bases for their raids on shipping and near-by settlements, and New Providence played an important role as a center of blockade-running operations during the Civil War in the United States. From this it might be assumed that the archipelago could be of great strategic value for naval and air bases from which an invader could launch attacks on the mainland, on Cuba, Jamaica, and Hispaniola, and on shipping between the United States and the Caribbean. This, however, is extremely doubtful, because of the lack of good harbors and of the difficulties that he would encounter in supplying materials for the construction work necessary to provide landing fields and seaplane bases for a large number of craft. Added to these difficulties would be the problem of fueling the planes and maintaining air and land crews. On the other hand, air bases of vital importance to the defense of the United States, Mexico, and the Greater Antilles and the guarding of the Windward Passage could be developed on these islands, since their accessibility from the Florida coast would make the matter of construction, maintenance, and supply a relatively simple matter.[1]

The Problem of Defense

Not only the Bahamas but many of the other European possessions as well as the United States possessions in the West Indies and the independent insular republics (Cuba, Haiti, and the Dominican Republic) are of great importance in the protection of the Panama Canal and the defense of the coast of the United States and the Caribbean mainland; and it would seem that no serious difficulties would be presented in establishing naval and air bases on those suited to the purpose and supplying provisions and replacements from the mainland.

The problem of defense in the Caribbean area has two aspects: the protection of shipping and the protection of the Panama Canal from destruction or seizure and of the rest of the mainland from invasion. The first of these is the lesser problem. If Britain is conquered, shipping in the Caribbean Sea would be reduced mainly to that between the United States and possibly Canada on the one hand and the Canal and the Caribbean islands and mainland on the other. It could consequently be confined to a minimum of routes in the Caribbean Sea and a single route to and from it by way of Florida Strait. Protective operations by sea and air could thus be closely concentrated.

Main Approaches to the Caribbean Sea

The problem of protection against attempts at invasion is much more difficult because of the large number of passages into the Caribbean Sea through the outer rim of islands. The more important of these from the standpoint of prewar use are: (1) Windward Passage between Cuba and the northern peninsula of Haiti (about 45 miles wide), (2) Mona Passage between the Dominican Republic and Puerto Rico (60 miles wide, but divided midway by Mona Island, a possession of the United States), (3) Anegada Passage (30 miles wide between the Virgin Islands and the lighthouse on the rock Sombrero, but 70 miles wide between the Virgin Islands and Anguilla Island of the British Leeward Islands Colony, the nearest island to the east from which defense operations could be carried on), and the unnamed southern passages (4) between the islands of Grenada and Tobago (about 85 miles wide) and (5) between Tobago and Trinidad (21 miles wide). In addition to these there are passages between all the larger islands of the chain that reaches from Anegada Passage to Grenada, six of which are from 10 to 30 miles wide, and three more than 25 miles

[1] The defense area in the Bahamas leased to the United States is the waters of Abraham Bay on Mayaguana Island and a small adjacent land area. Mayaguana Island (21 miles long, thickly wooded, generally low except for a few hills, of which the highest is 110 feet; population about 500) is at the southeast end of the archipelago between Mayaguana and Caicos Passages. Abraham Bay, on the south side, is about 5 miles wide and cannot be used by large ships, since it is enclosed by reefs through which there are only two passages, with depths of 12 feet and 6 to 8 feet, respectively.

wide. Particularly difficult also to guard, it would seem, would be the 65-mile stretch of the Grenadines between St. Vincent and Grenada, with their many narrow but deep passages and their numerous small harbors and shelters.

WINDWARD, JAMAICA, AND MONA PASSAGES

Only 85 miles from the mid-point of the Windward Passage is the United States Naval Reserve at Guantánamo Bay on the south coast of Cuba, which has been maintained as a small naval station since the Spanish-American War and is capable of development into a strong sea and air base. Kingston Harbor, which has long been the principal naval base of Great Britain in the Caribbean (the government drydock at Port Royal in this harbor is large enough for vessels of destroyer size) is about the same distance from the mid-point of Jamaica Passage (between Jamaica and the southern peninsula of Haiti), by which shipping through the Windward Passage continues on into the Caribbean Sea.[2] Protection for Mona Passage does not involve the use of any of the foreign possessions. In addition to the excellent harbor at San Juan, where there is a United States Naval Station with an airport for land planes and an established seaplane anchorage, Puerto Rico has a number of other fairly good harbors on both the north and south coasts, and Mayaguez Bay, directly facing the passage, has a 1250-foot wharf with 30 feet of water alongside and an anchorage suitable for emergency use by seaplanes. Mona Island —a low island 7 miles long by 4 wide—in the center of the passage might be suitable for an airplane base.

ANEGADA PASSAGE AND THE VIRGIN ISLANDS

The guarding of Anegada Passage would probably also not involve the use of bases on any of the present foreign possessions adjacent to it, although it would be imperative that these did not fall into the hands of the invader. Great Harbor on Culebra Island, a United States possession about 20 miles east of Puerto Rico and 100 miles northwest of the narrowest part of Anegada Passage, is already a "defensive sea area." On St. Thomas Island of the United States Virgin Islands, St. Thomas Harbor, about 23 miles west of Great Harbor, is a naval station and an established seaplane anchorage, and at Lindbergh Bay is a naval aviation landing field. St. Croix Island, which belongs to the United States Virgin Islands group but is separated from the other islands by a channel 40 miles wide, would seem to be in a particularly strategic position, since it directly faces the Anegada Passage. No harbors here can be rated as first class, but Christiansted Harbor, on the north side facing the passage, and Frederiksted Harbor, on the west end, have good anchorages, and there are United States naval radio stations at both harbors. The island is without established landing fields or seaplane anchorages, but there are emergency landing fields at both Christiansted and Frederiksted, that at Christiansted being a

---

[2] The defense sites on Jamaica leased by Great Britain to the United States include a fleet anchorage in Portland Bight, near-by land areas for landing fields and recreational and hospital facilities, and defense battery sites at entrances to the bight. The right to develop the Port Royal dockyard in Kingston Harbor for joint use by British and American forces is also granted. Portland Bight, about 15 miles east of Kingston, is a large open bay, 11¼ miles across and 8 miles deep. It is protected across the front by numerous reefs and cays, between which are channels passable by ships of deepest draft.

municipal field with some facilities that could probably be developed. There is also an emergency seaplane anchorage in Christiansted Harbor.

Even though the Anegada Passage could be guarded from these present possessions of the United States, the importance of the British Virgin Islands for both defense and invasion should not be lost sight of. These islands lie at the northeast corner of the Caribbean rim, not far from United States naval bases on St. Thomas Island and Culebra and from Puerto Rico and the rest of the Greater Antilles. Only Anegada, the most northeasterly, has any possibilities for the development of a landing field of any great size. The island is 9 miles long by 1 to 2 miles wide, low (almost uniformly 30 feet high), and, though covered with brushwood, could be cleared. No local supplies in any quantity are available, and, although water can be obtained by digging wells, the inhabitants depend largely on stored rain water. The local labor supply would be negligible. The interior of the southern end of the island and the north-central section is occupied by large salt-water lagoons, which might possibly be used as seaplane bases. Approaches to the island on all sides are menaced by reefs, and there is no anchorage that is safe except in light weather. Virgin Gorda, the next large island southeastward from Anegada, has two excellent anchorages on the west side for vessels of any draft. The north-ernmost of these, the bay between Mountain Point and Colison Point, is partially protected by the off-lying Dog Islands and might have possibilities for a large seaplane anchorage. Gorda Sound, on the north coast, is an "excellent and capacious harbor," 1¾ miles east and west and 1500 yards wide, with an average depth of 11 fathoms, and is sheltered from all winds. Water and some food supplies would be available, but the labor supply would be very small. Tortola, the largest and most populous island and the one nearest the United States, has no really good harbor. The anchorage for deep-draft vessels at Roadtown is an open roadstead, but the protected inner anchorage could probably be developed into a small seaplane base.

Anegada Passage to Guadeloupe

The British islands Anguilla and Barbuda, on the extreme eastern edge of the island groups immediately across Anegada Passage from the Virgin Islands, appear on the map as natural outposts for defense or among the first positions to attract the eye of an invader. Neither, however, has any good anchorages, fringing coral reefs make both difficult of approach, and on both fresh water is scarce and food supplies extremely limited. On Anguilla, only the small Road Bay is at all suitable for a seaplane anchorage and, while it would probably be possible to construct landing fields on this island, much clearing of scrub and leveling of the land would be necessary. At present there is no area on Barbuda that could be used even as an emergency landing field. In fact the island appears to offer no possibilities for the construction of a landing field of any large size: although the north, west, and south sides are low, they are very rough and covered with scrub. The long lagoon on the west side of the island (6 by 2 miles) might be used as a seaplane base. Although much of it is shallow there is a section 2½ miles long by 1 wide that is reported as suitable for seaplane landing. There would be considerable difficulty, however, in getting construction material and supplies into the lagoon owing to the fact that the water at the entrance is only two feet deep.

Of the other islands forming the outer border of the Lesser Antilles in this region, St. Martin (divided between the Netherlands and France) has a number of good anchorages, while the only harbor of any consequence on St. Barthélemy (French), Port de Gustavia, is of use only for small vessels. Two areas on St. Martin (at Grande Case Bay and at Marigot Bay) are suitable for emergency landing fields at the present time, and one on St. Barthélemy at St. Jean Bay is described as excellent, but there are no facilities at any of these fields. On St. Martin there is a radio station at Grande Case Bay and radio connection at Marigot Bay through this station. Both these bays are on the French part of the island. St. Barthélemy has no radio station.

Antigua is one of the islands on which the United States has leased sites from Great Britain for defense bases.[3] It has a number of bays, but most of them are too shallow for any but light-draft vessels, and almost the whole island is surrounded by dangerous reefs and shoals. Even the best harbors, St. John's on the north side and English on the south, are not suitable for large ships, although there are fairly well sheltered roadsteads at both. St. John's Harbor once had a naval dockyard but it has long been dismantled except the wharf, at which ships of draft up to 17 feet can still dock. There is an established seaplane anchorage at St. John's Harbor, and a number of other bays afford at least emergency anchorage. Antigua is without an established landing field, and it seems doubtful if any part of the island is really suitable for the construction of fields adequate for military purposes, since the only field now reported as suitable for even emergency landing is a large, rough moor about 3 miles east of St. John's. There is a radio station at St. John's.

The volcanic islands that form the inner chain of islands in this part of the Lesser Antilles—the Dutch islands Saba and St. Eustatius and the British islands St. Christopher, Nevis, and Montserrat—have no good harbors, few really well sheltered roadsteads, and, apparently, no areas suitable for large landing fields.

GUADELOUPE, DOMINICA, AND MARTINIQUE

Guadeloupe (French), the next island to the south, is separated from Montserrat and Antigua by Guadeloupe Passage (about 30 miles wide at its narrowest part), the first important passage southward from Anegada Passage. Because of the limited possibilities offered by Antigua as a base for defense operations, it would seem that a base on Guadeloupe is vitally essential for the defense of this passage. Pointe-à-Pitre Harbor, on the south side of the island, and the broad Petit Cul-de-Sac basin, by which it opens to the sea, form one of the best harbors and road-steads in the West Indies. The Grand Cul-de-Sac, on the north side facing Guadeloupe Passage, could also accommodate a large fleet, but entrance to its bays and anchorages through the bordering reefs and shoals involves extremely careful navigation. Pan American Airways operates an established seaplane anchorage at Pointe-à-Pitre, and there would seem to be no reason why a seaplane base could not be established in one or more of the bays opening into the Grand Cul-de-Sac. There is no landing field on the island and the mountainous western half, Basse-Terre, would seem to offer no possibilities for constructing one. On Grande-Terre, the low eastern half of the island, adequate landing fields could undoubtedly be

[3] The site on Antigua leased by Great Britain to the United States is an area on Parham Sound on the northeast side of the island and the narrow Crabs Peninsula that encloses Parham Harbor on the east. The anchorage in Parham Sound, which is about 1500 yards east and west and 880 yards north and south and which has depths of 3 to 7 fathoms, can accommodate only a few large ships at a time. Parham Harbor is available only to vessels of not more than 13-foot draft.

developed without too great difficulty. There is a radio station at Pointe-à-Pitre. The small islands and groups of islands a few miles off the south coast of Guadeloupe—Les Saintes, Marie-Galante, and others—would form something of an outer line of defense for craft using Pointe-à-Pitre Harbor as a base, and the low, round Marie-Galante (about 8 miles in diameter) might have possibilities for an airplane base, although its position would make it extremely vulnerable from the Atlantic.

Dominica Passage, the 13-mile-wide channel between the islands off the south coast of Guadeloupe and the British island of Dominica, could be guarded from a base at Pointe-à-Pitre. Dominica itself would probably be of little value to either defender or invader. It has no good harbors, no places where well sheltered seaplane bases could be established, and probably no areas suitable for a landing field adequate for military purposes. On the other hand, the French island of Martinique, to the south, is not only in a strategic position between the 22-mile-wide Martinique Passage on the north and the 17-mile-wide St. Lucia Channel on the south, but has in Fort-de-France Bay one of the best harbors in the Caribbean. Evidence of the strategic importance of Fort-de-France Bay is to be had from the fact that France was able to hold Martinique almost continuously from the time that the first settlements were made on it and that it was the base from which the French were able many times to raid successfully other European possessions in the Caribbean. Since the fall of France in the present war there have been rumors that the Vichy government intends to refortify the bay. An established seaplane anchorage at Fort-de-France is operated by Pan American Airways, and a number of other bays would afford shelter for ships and seaplanes, but there is no established landing field and no area well suited for one unless one or more of the few sugar plantations on level ground at delta heads should be taken over for the purpose. There is a radio station at Fort-de-France.

St. Lucia to Grenada

Probably quite as important as Fort-de-France Bay as a base for guarding the passages into the Caribbean in this part of the Lesser Antilles is Port Castries on the next island to the south, the British island of St. Lucia, another of the British possessions on which sites for defense bases have been leased by the United States.[4] Port Castries is a landlocked harbor averaging a quarter of a mile wide and extending a mile into the island. With depths of 4 to 10 fathoms over most of its area, it is available at all times for all classes of ships. Of several wharves one is 650 feet long and has depths of 23 to 30 feet alongside. No landing field exists on the island at present, but there is an established seaplane anchorage at Port Castries, and a number of other bays on the island would shelter seaplanes and a limited number of deep-draft ships. There is a radio station at Port Castries.

From St. Lucia to Trinidad, where the United States has also leased a site or sites for a defense base, is a distance of about 225 miles. St. Vincent Passage (24 miles wide), between St. Lucia and St. Vincent, could be guarded from bases on St.

4 The defense site on St. Lucia leased by Great Britain to the United States is an area of approximately 120 acres in Gros Islet Bay for a seaplane base. This bay is on the west side of the island about 4 miles northward from Port Castries, with which it is connected by a good road. It lies between Pigeon Island on the north and Fourreur on the south (1 ¼ miles apart). There are anchorages for ships of any draft at the west end of Pigeon Island and in Ste. Croix Roads south of the island.

Lucia, but the many narrow, though navigable, passages through the 65-mile chain of the Grenadines (British), between St. Vincent and Grenada, would probably present a serious patrol and defense problem, particularly with the opportunities for concealment afforded by the numerous islands and rocks composing the chain and the many harbors where one or more ships could shelter. St. Vincent (British) has little to offer as a base for defense. It has no good harbors, and the best, Kingstown Bay, is hardly to be recommended even as a base for seaplanes. Though sheltered from the trade winds, it is open to the south and west, and down-valley winds frequently blow into it with great violence. Owing to the ruggedness of the island there are reported to be no areas at present that could be safely used for landing airplanes.

Grenada (British) seems worthy of consideration for the establishment of at least a small base, from which assistance could be given to the defense base on St. Lucia in guarding the Grenadine passages and to the defense base on Trinidad in guarding the 72-mile passage between the two islands. The only good harbor, St. George's, on the southwest side, can accommodate only a small number of ships of deep draft or great length. Although all of the three basins comprising the harbor are deep enough for ships of any draft, only one of them is large enough for ships to lie safe unless moored both head and stern. The island lacks an established seaplane anchorage or landing field, but St. George's Harbor should afford good shelter for seaplanes, and Queen's Park (2297 by 1312 feet) near the town of St. George's can be used as an emergency landing field and could probably be improved. There is a radio station at St. George's.

BARBADOS, TOBAGO, AND TRINIDAD

Except that its isolated position would make it extremely vulnerable to attack by enemy warcraft, Barbados (British) would seem to be ideally located for an outpost from which a lookout from the air could be maintained for warcraft heading toward the passages into the Caribbean between Guadeloupe and Grenada. The only ship anchorage of any importance, however, is at Carlisle Bay on the southwest side, and it would not be suitable for either a ship or seaplane base. Although somewhat sheltered from the trade winds, this bay is exposed to the south, west, and northwest. There is an established commercial landing field at Bridgetown on Carlisle Bay— the only one between Puerto Rico and Trinidad— and the topography of the island suggests that there are other areas on which landing fields could be laid out. Bridgetown is a center for radio and cable communications in this part of the Caribbean.

Tobago (British) has a number of fairly well sheltered anchorages which might be used as patrol and defense outposts in connection with a naval and air base on Trinidad. It has no established landing fields or seaplane bases, but it would seem that there might be sites for landing fields on the low plain at the southwest end of the island, while both Buccoo Lagoon on the northwest side of the island and King's Bay on the southeast side would afford well sheltered anchorages for seaplanes with fairly long take-offs within the harbors.

Trinidad (British), on which the United States has leased a site or sites yet to be designated for a defense base, has no good anchorages except in the Gulf of Paria. This gulf is, however, a great landlocked basin: the section embraced between the peninsulas at the north and south extremities of the west side of the island is nearly 50 miles long and averages about 24 miles wide. The natural defenses against invasion afforded by the north and south entrances to the Gulf could be further strengthened by fortifications. The four narrow channels that form the northern entrance (The Dragons' Mouths) are all passable for deep-draft ships, although their navigation could be improved by dredging and blasting in certain sections. The single southern entrance channel (The Serpent's Mouth) can be used now only by ships of moderate draft. The anchorage at Port of Spain is safe in all seasons and the port works, now nearing completion there, will provide wharfage for ships of draft up to nearly 30 feet at low-water level. Fuel and gasoline would be available in any quantity required. There is at present an airport 10 miles southeast of Port of Spain and an established seaplane anchorage and station at Cocorite Bay just south of the town. Other landing fields and seaplane bases could be established.[5]

THE GUIANAS

None of the Guianas—British, Netherlands, or French—have harbors suitable for naval bases. The only anchorages are at the mouths of the large rivers, and these cannot accommodate deep-draft ships. Bases for aircraft could be established at numerous points along the Guiana coast[6]—seaplane anchorages at river mouths and landing fields on the low coastal plain—and might be of importance in patrolling and guarding the southern approaches to the Caribbean. Cayenne (French Guiana), however, is more than 700 miles from Trinidad, Paramaribo (Netherlands Guiana) 500 miles, and Georgetown (British Guiana) more than 200 miles. These distances are also to be considered in weighing the possibility of an invader using the Guianas as stepping stones for a large-scale invasion of the Caribbean or for striking at the Panama Canal.

CURAÇAO, ARUBA, AND BONAIRE

The Dutch islands off the coast of Venezuela—Curaçao, Aruba, and Bonaire—might be considered important as a second line of defense against invasion by way of the southern passage into the Caribbean between Grenada and Trinidad. This would probably be the most difficult to defend of all the passages. Not only is it the most distant from the United States, but it is the widest entrance to the Caribbean. In amount of traffic carried in normal times it is second only to the Windward Passage and is much more vulnerable, since defense bases in the Bahamas and on Jamaica, together with the present naval base at Guantánamo, will provide three lines of defense for the Windward Passage.

The largest island, Curaçao, has several harbors on the leeward southwest side. Santa Anna Bay, the harbor of Willemstad, consists of a channel, 110 to 325 yards wide and 1650 yards long, and a wide inner bay, the Schottegat, which is bordered by islands and reefs but has a clear central anchorage about 325 yards in diameter. The channel has a least depth of about 45 feet, and the greater part of the Schottegat

5 At the time this section is written (December 17, 1940) the site for the defense base on Trinidad has not been agreed on. The United States government desires a site in and on the Gulf of Paria, and the government of the colony wishes to assign one on swampy, uninhabited land on the south coast.

6 Two sites for defense bases in British Guiana have been leased by Great Britain to the United States. Both are for air bases—a patrol-squadron base with an aerodrome on the Demerara River 25 miles above its mouth and a seaplane base near Suddie on the west bank of the mouth of the Essequibo River.

is from 8 to 11 fathoms deep. There are a number of wharves with depths of 18 to 30 feet alongside. Caracas Bay, five miles to the southeast, has three wharves that can accommodate ships of the largest size. On Aruba, Paarden Bay, the harbor of Oranjestad, can be entered only by ships of not more than 20-foot draft, but St. Nicolaas Bay, near the southern end of the island, has a least depth at the entrance of 41 feet. There are no harbors on Bonaire. Curaçao and Aruba have each a government and commercial airport, and there is an established seaplane anchorage in the Schottegat on Curaçao. Aruba has no established seaplane anchorage, but the lagoons on the south side of the island can be used as emergency anchorages. There is no anchorage on Bonaire suitable for seaplanes and only a dangerous emergency landing field. Fuel oil and aviation gasoline would be available on both Curaçao and Aruba in any required quantity as long as the refineries were kept in operation and access to the source of crude oil supply in the Maracaibo Basin maintained.

Venezuelan, Colombian, and Nicaraguan Islands

Also to be considered for their strategic importance in the defense of the Caribbean area are two groups of islands that are territories of near-by mainland republics—the Venezuelan islands between Trinidad and Bonaire and the Colombian and Nicaraguan islands off the coast of Nicaragua. The Venezuelan islands might be used with the Dutch islands as a second line of defense for the entrance into the Caribbean between Grenada and Trinidad. Many of them are mere rocky islets, and even on the larger of them there are no harbors suitable for large ships, although Margarita, Los Testigos, Coche, Tortuga, Blanquilla, and Los Roques have good anchorages for large ships and harbors suitable for seaplane anchorages. There are radio stations on Margarita and Los Roques. Only on Margarita, the largest island (population about 70,000), would there be any considerable labor force available for employment in defense construction and maintenance.

The Colombian and Nicaraguan islands, cays, and banks off the coast of Nicaragua have long been considered of strategic importance in connection with the proposed Nicaraguan canal. They also lie close to the shipping route to the Panama Canal by way of the Windward Passage, and the southernmost islands of the archipelago are less than 250 miles from Colón. Formerly Colombia claimed the whole archipelago but seems now to have relinquished her claim to Great and Little Corn Islands, which Nicaragua leased to the United States in connection with the Convention of 1914 respecting the Nicaraguan canal route. Colombia still claims the rest of the archipelago, administering it as the Intendencia of San Andrés and Providencia (see below page 98) and disputing the right of the United States to Serrana and Quita Sueño Banks and Roncador Cay, of which it took possession in 1919 under authority of an act of Congress of 1856 dealing with unoccupied guano islands. San Andrés and Providencia, the largest islands and the only ones permanently inhabited, have each a good harbor, but only for ships of up to 15-foot draft. There are, however, a number of good anchorages, although the many banks and reefs make navigation somewhat dangerous for large ships. The harbors on San Andrés and Providencia might be suitable for seaplane bases. There would be a considerable labor supply (total population in 1938, 6528).

BALANCE OF TRADE AND FISCAL POSITION OF THE EUROPEAN POSSESSIONS IN THE CARIBBEAN AREA

Table XV presents a general view of the balance of trade of the European possessions in the Caribbean Area during recent years and of the fiscal position of the British and Netherlands possessions. It should be noted that the data in this table have been derived in some instances from other sources than those used in the preparation of the text and do not always correspond precisely with the latter.

It may be determined from the table that, of the British possessions, only the Leeward Islands Colony as a whole, Grenada in the Windward Islands, and British Guiana had trade balances that were predominantly favorable during the five-year period 1934–1938, the annual average excess of exports over imports being, respectively, $178,000, $1000, and $2,002,000. All the British colonies together experienced an adverse trade balance averaging $14,728,000 annually during the five-year period and amounting in 1938 to $17,498,000. On the other hand, the governments of the colonies as a group more than met expenditures with revenue during the five-year period, when the excess of revenues over expenditures averaged $2,484,000 each year; in 1938, however, there was a total deficit for all the colonies of about $47,000. The combined deficits of the governments of the Bahama Islands, Dominica, St. Lucia, Grenada, and British Honduras averaged $220,000 annually in the period 1934–1938, but in 1938 the total deficit of these governments increased to $1,446,000, largely on account of heavy expenditures incurred in the Bahama Islands in that year.

The trade of the Netherlands possessions was of considerably greater value than that of all the British possessions put together for the five-year period 1934–1938 and in 1938 its value was a little more than twice as great. This, of course, is due entirely to the important oil refineries on the islands of Curaçao and Aruba. The Netherlands possessions experienced an adverse balance of trade of about $26,586,000 in 1938; the much smaller average annual adverse balance for the five-year period ($5,095,000), however, is explained by the fact that the trade balance for Curaçao was consistently favorable in 1934, 1935, and 1936. The balance for Surinam was adverse in all five years except 1937. During the four-year period 1934–1937 for the Territory of Curaçao the average annual excess of revenue over expenditures was about $635,000, but in Surinam the average annual deficit during the same period was about $1,695,000.

The French possessions as a whole enjoyed a favorable trade balance averaging about $4,600,000 each year during the period 1934–1937 and totaling about $2,000,000 in 1937. For French Guiana, however, the balance has been adverse, averaging about $1,000,000 annually for the four-year period and amounting to some $600,000 in 1937. Comparative statistics for revenues and expenditures for the French colonies were not available.

TABLE XV—EUROPEAN POSSESSIONS IN THE CARIBBEAN AREA: IMPORTS, EXPORTS, AND GOVERNMENTAL REVENUES AND EXPENDITURES, ANNUAL AVERAGES FOR THE PERIOD 1934–1938 (OR 1934–1937) AND TOTALS FOR 1938 (OR 1937)

(Values in thousands of United States dollars)

	Imports		Exports		Revenues		Expenditures	
	Average 1934–38 a=1934 -1937	1938 b=1937	Average 1934–38 a=1934 -1937	1938 b=1937	Average 1934–38 a=1934 -1937	1938	Average 1934–38 a=1934 -1937	1938
British Possessions	93,979	109,392	79,251	91,894	40,782	46,146	38,298	46,193
Bahama Islands	4,732	5,608	732	1,058	1,837	2,013	1,944	3,205
Jamaica	26,358	30,788	20,614	24,607	11,784	13,887	11,639	13,954
Leeward Islands Colony	2,705	3,074	2,883	2,532	1,249	1,455	1,169	1,401
Br. Virgin Islands	54	69	50	48	39	44	30	33
St. Christopher-Nevis	1,313	1,476	1,487	1,302	572	672	514	600
Montserrat	276	289	270	202	138	133	145	182
Antigua	1,062	1,240	1,076	980	500	606	480	586
Windward Islands	3,918	3,839	3,371	3,779	1,994	2,062	2,025	2,159
Dominica	580	503	319	379	368	360	381	387
St. Lucia	981	926	849	831	431	433	448	486
St. Vincent	902	972	747	1,030	431	499	424	473
Grenada	1,455	1,438	1,456	1,539	764	770	772	813
Barbados	9,943	10,123	7,023	6,597	2,554	2,736	2,417	2,738
Trinidad and Tobago	33,091	41,137	30,263	36,756	13,179	15,883	11,620	14,448
British Guiana	10,063	10,819	12,065	13,302	6,870	6,369	6,094	6,416
British Honduras	3,169	4,004	2,300	3,263	1,315	1,741	1,390	1,872
Netherlands Possessions	147,914	217,695	142,819	191,107	a8,156	8,251	a9,290	9,152
Terr. of Curaçao	144,207	214,920	139,472	187,471	a5,676	5,914	a5,041	5,411
Surinam	3,707	3,775	3,347	3,636	2,453	2,337	4,148	3,741
French Possessions	a20,200	b20,700	a24,800	b22,700				
Martinique	9,400	7,500	10,400	8,100				
Guadeloupe and Dependencies	8,600	8,500	11,300	11,900				
French Guiana	a2,600	b2,100	a1,600	b1,500				

The table is based on the following sources: *British possessions*: "Dominions Office List, 1940"; *Territory of Curaçao*, exports and imports: "League of Nations Statistical Yearbook, 1933–1939," p. 210; revenues and expenditures: 1934–1937, "Curaçaosch Verslag," 1938, Part II, p. 7; 1938, "Statesman's Yearbook," 1940; *Surinam*, exports and imports: "Statesman's Yearbook," 1936, 1938, 1939, 1940; revenues and expenditures, 1934–1937: "Surinamsch Verslag," 1938, Part I, p. 7; 1938, data furnished by courtesy of the Netherlands Information Bureau, New York; *Martinique and Guadeloupe*: "League of Nations Statistical Yearbook," 1938–1939, p. 218; *French Guiana*: "U. S. Department of Commerce, Foreign Commerce Yearbook," 1938, p. 422.

Values given in pounds and guilders in the above sources have been converted into current U. S. dollars by multiplying them by the average annual exchange rates as given in the "Federal Reserve Bulletin" (see p. v); those given in U. S. gold dollars (all data for the French possessions) were multiplied by 1.6932 (i. e. $1.00 divided by $0.5906, the gold content of the dollar since January 31, 1934), and the product was then rounded to the nearest $100,000.

NOTE ON THE ISLAND TERRITORIES OF COLOMBIA AND VENEZUELA

INTENDENCIA OF SAN ANDRÉS AND PROVIDENCIA

Government. The archipelago of San Andrés belongs to the Republic of Colombia and is governed directly from Bogotá as the Intendencia of San Andrés and Providencia. The highest authority is the Intendente, appointed by the President of the Republic. He has both executive and legislative powers, and is responsible only to the national executive. A measure of authority is vested in local municipal councils, elected by popular vote. Seat of government and chief municipality: San Andrés, on San Andrés Island.

Physical Features. Situated directly north of the Panama Canal, off the east coasts of Nicaragua and Honduras, the archipelago consists of seven groups of coral reefs and cays and two small islands (total land area, 21 sq. mi.). The largest island, San Andrés, is about 7 miles long and from three-quarters of a mile to one and one-half miles wide and reaches maximum elevations of slightly more than 300 feet. Providencia Island, 48 miles north of San Andrés, is volcanic in origin, with an extremely rugged interior, rising to elevations of more than 1000 feet. Both San Andrés and Providencia are surrounded by fringing coral cays and reefs.

None of the other coral reefs, cays, and dry sand banks rise to more than 35 feet above the sea. They are generally barren, although scattered samphire grass, brushwood, and occasional coconut palms are found on some of them.

History. San Andrés and Providencia long served as bases for the operations of pirates. Throughout most of the nineteenth century and the first quarter of the twentieth, ownership was in dispute between Colombia and Nicaragua. In 1930 a treaty was ratified in which Nicaragua finally recognized the sovereignty of Colombia (see also above, p. 95).

Population. San Andrés and Providencia are the only permanently inhabited islands, although other cays and reefs are visited periodically by fishermen. According to the census of the Colombian Republic in 1938, the total population was 6528 (St. Andrés, 4261; Providencia, 2267). The inhabitants are almost entirely English-speaking West Indian Negroes and mulattoes (descendants of slaves brought here by the pirates).

Production and Trade. The principal industries are farming, stock raising, and fishing. The leading exports are coconuts, oranges, coconut oil, and copra. The total value of the exports, which go largely to Cartagena and Barranquilla, is almost three times the total value of the imports.

Communications. Rough trail-like roads are found on San Andrés and Providencia. San Andrés village, on San Andrés Island, and Santa Isabel village on Providencia are frequently visited by the moderate-sized vessels which carry on the trade of the islands.

NUEVA ESPARTA

Government. Nueva Esparta is one of twenty autonomous and politically equal states composing the United States of Venezuela. Under a constitution modeled on that of the nation, it elects its own Legislative Assembly and President. Suffrage is limited to men over 21 years of age. Capital: La Asunción on Margarita Island.

Physical Features. Of the many islands and cays that make up the state of Nueva Esparta and extend for a distance of about 320 miles along the north coast of Venezuela, Margarita Island is by far the largest and most important. Geologically an outlying segment of the coast range of Venezuela, this island (444 sq. mi.) has two rugged mountainous halves, joined by a low sandy isthmus. The highest peak in the western part rises to 3806 feet, and that in the eastern to 3240 feet. The other islands are much smaller; comparatively low, they are generally composed of coralliferous limestones capping a basement of older rocks. In a few of them the granitic cores are exposed, as in one of the steep-sided islets of the Hermanos group, which attains an elevation of 650 feet, the highest point in the state outside of Margarita.

In the eastern part of Margarita there are springs in the mountains, and three of the five main valleys have permanent streams. However, water is either of poor quality or entirely lacking on all of the other islands. The fishermen who visit the many small islands sometimes obtain extremely brackish water from shallow wells, but more commonly they carry their water with them from Margarita or the Venezuelan mainland.

Climate and Vegetation. No official climatic data are available for any part of Nueva Esparta, but all of the islands are known to lie in the arid or semiarid zone of the north coast of South America. Although slight variations occur in response to differences in elevation and exposure, the total amount of rainfall is everywhere extremely small.

The drought-resistant vegetation, dominated by cactus, salicornia, and samphire, clearly reflects the high temperatures and meager rainfall. Mangrove swamps are found along the coasts and surrounding the many lagoons. The only island having enough water and sufficiently high elevations to give significant variations in the vegetation is Margarita, where the higher peaks have a forest cover.

History. Margarita was discovered and named by Columbus in 1498, and on Cubagua was built New Cadiz, the first white settlement in South America (1515). The early discovery of the pearl-oyster beds in the surrounding seas led to the settlement of the islands in the sixteenth century.

Although the merchants and sailors of Margarita played a role in the Venezuelan War of Independence, the historical importance of the islands has dwindled greatly in recent times, and the present contact of the inhabitants with the outside world is small.

Population. According to the Venezuelan census of 1936, the population of Nueva Esparta is 73,375. About 70,000 people live on Margarita, where the three principal settlements are the ports of Porlamar (5000) and Pampatar (1000) and the capital city, La Asunción (3000), in the interior. Coche, the third largest island in area, is second in population, with about 3000 inhabitants. Gran Roque had 320 permanent residents. On the other islands, including Tortuga (second in area), there are almost no inhabitants except occasional fishermen. The population is a mixture of whites, Indians, mulattoes, and Negroes. The universal language is Spanish.

Production and Trade. Although the pearling grounds around Margarita have been badly depleted, a large number of men are still employed in pearl fishing, and this industry even now affords the most important occupation in the island. The yearly export of pearls is valued at about $300,000. Hammocks, straw hats, embroideries, pottery, and roof tiles are made by the natives, and these, as well as goatskins, divi-divi beans, fish, and salt, are exported in substantial amounts. Along the northeastern coast near Manzanillo and Constanza an American syndicate is engaged in mining magnesite ore of unusual purity.

On the other islands fishing is the leading occupation. Salt is gathered on Coche and Orchilla, and goats and cattle are raised on Blanquilla and Los Testigos. Guano and phosphate deposits are known to exist on a number of the islands. The phosphates of Gran Roque have been worked from time to time since the middle of the nineteenth century, and there are undeveloped deposits of potential value on the southwestern side of the island. Sulphur is reported on Tortuga, and the possibility of oil on Cubagua has been suggested.

Communications. There are no established lines of communication on any of the islands except Margarita, and here there are only a few poor short roads on the eastern end of the island. Both Pampatar and Porlamar are visited frequently by vessels from ports along the mainland coast and Trinidad. Pampatar Bay affords anchorage for ships drawing 42 to 48 feet of water, and La Mar Bay, on which Porlamar is located, permits the anchorage of vessels of 27-foot draft. Porlamar is connected with Maracay, on the mainland of Venezuela, by a regular air service. There are good emergency seaplane anchorages at Tortuga, Los Roques, and Margarita.

LIST OF REFERENCES

With a few exceptions, this list includes only works actually used in the compilation of the present booklet and certain outstanding current bibliographies from which many additional titles may readily be obtained.

GENERAL WORKS

Current Bibliographies

Bibliographie géographique internationale. Paris, 1894–. (Annual.)
Current Geographical Publications. Amer. Geogr. Soc., New York, 1938–. (Mimeographed; monthly.)
Geographisches Jahrbuch. Gotha. (Annual. For references on the Caribbean area see especially Vols. 12, 1888; 14, 1890–1891; 16, 1893; 18, 1895; 20, 1897; 22, 1899; 25, 1902; 27, 1904; 30, 1907; 36, 1913; 41, 1926.)
Handbook of Latin American Studies. Cambridge, Massachusetts, 1936–. (Annual.)
The Pan American Bookshelf. Washington, 1938–. (Mimeographed; monthly.)

Yearbooks

The South American Handbook. . . London.
The Statesman's Year-Book, . . . London.
The West Indies Yearbook, Including also the Bermudas, the Bahamas, British Guiana, and British Honduras . . . [1939] Montreal.

Guide Books and Coast Pilots

ASPINALL, SIR E. *The Pocket Guide to the West Indies, British Guiana, Birtish Honduras, Bermuda, the Spanish Main, Surinam, and the Panama Canal* [1940]. New York. (Annual.)
OBER, F. S. A guide to the West Indies, Bermuda, and Panama. New York, 1920.
U. S. Bureau of Foreign and Domestic Commerce. Commercial travelers' guide to Latin America, 4th edition. (*Trade Promotion Series No. 122*), Washington, 1931.
U. S. Hydrographic Office. Sailing directions for east coasts of Central America and Mexico, including north coast of Colombia, 4th ed. (*H.O. No. 130*), Washington, 1939.
U. S. Hydrographic Office. Sailing directions for the West Indies, Vol. 1, Section B, Principal ports. (*H.O. No. 128*), Washington, 1936.
U. S. Hydrographic Office. West Indies pilot, Vol. 2, The Lesser Antilles and the coast of Venezuela, 4th ed. (*H.O. No. 129*), Washington, 1929.

Other General Works

DAVIS, W. M. The Lesser Antilles. (*Amer. Geogr. Soc. Map of Hispanic America Pub. No. 2.*) New York, 1926.
DIETRICH, GÜTHNER. Das Amerikanische Mittelmeer: ein meereskundlicher Überblick. *Zeitschr. Gesell. für Erdkunde zu Berlin*, Heft 3/4, Mai 1939, pp. 108–130.
ELIOT, G. F. The ramparts we watch. New York, 1939.
ELLIOTT, A. R. European colonies in the Western Hemisphere. (*Foreign Policy Reports*, Vol. 16, No. 11), New York, August, 1940.
HILL, R. T. Cuba and Porto Rico with the other islands of the West Indies: their topography, climate, flora, products, industries, cities, people, political conditions, etc. New York, 1898.
JONES, C. L. Caribbean backgrounds and prospects. New York, 1931.
KNOCH, K. Klimakunde von Südamerika. (Handbuch der Klimatologie, Band II, Teil G.) Berlin, 1930.
PLATT, R. R. A note on political sovereignty and administration in the Caribbean. *Geogr. Rev.*, Vol. 16, 1926, pp. 623–637.
REED, W. W. Climatological data for the West Indian islands. *Monthly Weather Rev.*, Vol. 54, 1926, pp. 133–160.

Sorre, Max. Les Antilles. *In his* Mexique, Amérique centrale. (Géographie Universelle, Vol. 14, pp. 149–222.) Paris, 1928.

Troll, Carl. Curaçao, Trinidad und Tobago. *In* Fritz Klute, Handbuch der geographischen Wissenschaft, Lief. 50, Süd Amerika. Heft 15, Potsdam, 1930.

U. S. Weather Bureau. *Climatological Data.* West Indies and Caribbean service. San Juan.

Vandercook, J. W. Caribbee cruise; a book of the West Indies. New York, 1938.

BRITISH COLONIES
General Works

Great Britain. *Colonial Reports—Annual.* London. (Each report bears the title: "Annual report on the social and economic progress of the people of. . . ." See the following sections of this list for references to the reports used in preparation of this work.)

Great Britain, Dept. of Overseas Trade. Report on economic and commercial conditions in the British West Indies, British Guiana, British Honduras, and Bermuda 1937, by W. D. Lambie and C. M. Pickthall. (*[Reports] No. 688*), London.

Macmillan, W. M. Warning from the West Indies: a tract for Africa and the Empire. London, [1935].

Moyne, W. E. G. The West Indies in 1939. *Geogr. Journ.*, Vol. 96, 1940, pp. 85–92.

Orde-Browne, G. St. J., Labor conditions in the West Indies. (*Cmd. 6070*), London, 1939.

Report of the West Indian Sugar Commission. Presented by the Secretary of State for the Colonies to Parliament by command of His Majesty, March, 1930. (*Cmd. 3517*), London, 1930.

The Dominions Office and Colonial Office List. London. (Annual.)

Warrington, George. The West Indies, with British Guiana and British Honduras. New York, 1925.

West Indian Royal Commission, 1938–1939. Recommendations, presented by the Secretary of State for the Colonies to Parliament by command of His Majesty, February, 1940. (*Cmd. 6174*), London, 1940.

Bahama Islands and Jamaica

Corfield, G. S. Sponge industry of the Caribbean area. *Econ. Geogr.*, Vol. 14, 1935, pp. 201–206.

Great Britain. *Colonial Reports—Annual, No. 1901* [on Bahama Islands, 1938], 1939.

Moseley, Mary. The Bahamas Handbook. Nassau, 1926.

Nassau, Bahama, Development Board. The Bahama Islands: information as to trade, soil, climate, etc., for intending settlers, tourists, and business men. Nassau, 1928.

Shattuck, G. B. The Bahama Islands. (The Geographical Society of Baltimore.) New York, 1905.

Cundall, Frank. *The Handbook of Jamaica* . . . [1936] . . . Kingston. (Annual.)

Great Britain. *Colonial Reports—Annual, No. 1896* [on Jamaica, 1938], 1939.

Hill, R. T. The geology and physical geography of Jamaica: a study of a type of Antillean development. *Bull. Museum of Comp. Zoöl. of Harvard Coll.*, Vol. 34, Geol. ser., Vol. 4. Cambridge, Massachusetts, 1899.

Olivier, S. H. O. Jamaica, the blessed island. London, [1936].

Leeward and Windward Islands

Great Britain. *Colonial Reports—Annual, No. 1923* [on Grenada, 1937 and 1938], 1939; *No. 1929* [on St. Lucia, 1938], 1940; *No. 1933* [on St. Vincent, 1938], 1940; *No. 1934* [on the Leeward Islands, 1938], 1940.

Guppy, R. J. L. On the geology of Antigua and other West Indian islands with reference to the physical history of the Caribean [!] region. *Quart. Journ. Geol. Soc.*, Vol. 67, No. 268, 1911, pp. 681–700.

The Grenada Handbook, Directory, and Almanac . . . [1927], compiled by the Colonial Secretary. London. (Annual.)

Watkins, F. H. Handbook of the Leeward Islands. London, 1924.

Barbados, Trinidad and Tobago

Great Britain. *Colonial Reports—Annual, No. 1913* [on Barbados, 1938–1939], 1939.
Sinckler, E. G. The Barbados handbook. London, 1914.
Starkey, O. P. The economic geography of Barbados: a study of the relationships between environmental variations and economic development. New York, 1939.
Great Britain. *Colonial Reports—Annual, No. 1891* [on Trinidad and Tobago, 1937], 1939.
James, P. E. A geographic reconnaissance of Trinidad. *Econ. Geogr.*, Vol. 3, 1927, pp. 87–109.
Liddle, R. A. The geology of Venezuela and Trinidad. Fort Worth, [1928].
Shephard, C. Y. The sugar industry of the British West Indies and British Guiana with special reference to Trinidad. *Econ. Geogr.*, Vol. 5, 1929, pp. 149–175.
Skutsch, Ilse. Die Inseln Trinidad und Tobago: Landeskundliche Darstellung einer britischen Kolonie. Engelsdorf, Leipzig, 1929.

British Guiana and British Honduras

Francis, William, and John Mullin. The British Guiana handbook, 1922. Georgetown, [1923].
Great Britain. *Colonial Reports—Annual, No. 1926* [on British Guiana, 1938], 1940.
Litchfield, Lawrence, Jr. Bauxite mining in British Guiana. *Engineering and Mining Journ.*, Vol. 128, 1929, pp. 346–349.
Report of the British Guiana Commission to the President's Advisory Committee on Political Refugees. [Washington?, 1939.]
Webber, A. R. F. Centenary history and handbook of British Guiana. [Georgetown], 1931.

Dunlop, W. R. Report on the economic and natural features of British Honduras in relation to agriculture, with proposals for development. London, [1922].
Great Britain. *Colonial Reports—Annual, No. 1894* [on British Honduras, 1938], 1939.
Metzgen, M. S. and *H. E. Cain.* The handbook of British Honduras, comprising historical, statistical, and general information concerning the colony. London, 1925.

FRENCH COLONIES
General

Grandidier, G., ed. Atlas des colonies françaises . . . Paris, 1934.
Le Tricentenaire des Antilles françaises. *L'Illustration*, Vol. 93, No. 4838, Nov., 1935.
Martinique, Guadeloupe, Guyane, St. Pierre-Miquelon. (*Guides des colonies françaises.*) Paris, 1931.
Rodway, James. Guiana: British, Dutch, and French. New York, 1912.

Martinique

Annuaire de la vie martiniquaise. [1936]. Fort-de-France, Martinique.
Debretagne, L. Labour conditions in Martinique. *Internatl. Labour Rev.*, Vol. 32, 1935, pp. 792–800.
Giraud, J. Equisse géologique de la Martinique, avec carte géologique. Hanoi-Haiphong, 1918.
Perret, F. A. The eruption of Mont Pelée, 1929–1932. (*Carnegie Inst. of Washington, Publ. 458.*) 1935.
Rejon, A. La Martinique. Paris, 1928.
Romer, A. Étude sur la climatologie de la colonie. (Martinique, Service de Méteorologie.) Fort-de-France, Martinique, 1933.

Guadeloupe

Commerce 1936 à la Guadeloupe. *Colonies autonomes*, Sept., 1937, pp. 29–30.

Grébert, René. Les forêts de la Guadeloupe. *Bull. de l' Agence Econ. des Colonies Autonomes*, Vol. 27, 1934, pp. 639–702, 765–876, 941–1015.

La Guadeloupe. *Bull. de l'Agence Générale des Colonies*, Vol. 20, 1927, pp. 203–216, 395–407.

La Guadeloupe et ses dépendances. *Colonies autonomes*, Dec., 1935, pp. 149–159.

Rigotard, Marcel. Une vieille colonie agricole: la Guadeloupe. *L'Agriculture pratique des pays chauds*, Vol. 1, 1930, pp. 182–193.

Stehlé, H. Flore de la Guadeloupe et dépendances. Tome Ier, Essai d'écologie et de géographie botanique. Basse-Terre, Martinique, 1935.

French Guiana

Adam, D. El Dorado, la Guyane française agricole. Paris, 1936.

Commerce 1936 de la Guyane. *Colonies autonomes*, Juin, 1937, pp. 19–20.

Devez, G. Les plantes utiles et bois industriels de la Guyane. *L'Agriculture pratique des pays chauds*, Vol. 3, 1932, pp. 133–148, 303–314.

Jameau, Jean. La Guyane française. [Paris], 1935.

Lacroix, A. Guyane française. *In* La Géologie et les mines de la France d'outre-mer. Paris, 1932.

La Guyane et le territoire de l'Inini. *Colonies autonomes*, Dec., 1935, pp. 173–183.

La Guyane française. *Bull. de l'Agence Générale des Colonies*, Vol. 20, 1927, pp. 743–757, 927–952.

L'Exploitation forestière en Guyane française. *Bull. de l'Agence Générale des Colonies*, Vol. 22, 1929, pp. 955–965.

Clipperton Island

Le drapeau français sur Clipperton. *L'Illustration*, Vol. 93, 1935, pp. 262–263.

Pelleray, E. Clipperton. *L'Océanie française*, Vol. 27, 1931, pp. 4–5.

Regelsperger, G. L'île Clipperton, définitivement reconnue française. *Rev. générale des sciences pures et appliquées*, Vol. 42, 1931, pp. 421–422.

U. S. Hydrographic Office. Mexico and Central America (West Coast). Seventh edition. (*H.O. No. 84*), Washington, 1928, pp. 67–68.

Veyrie, J. la. Le passage du croiseur "Jeanne d'Arc" à l'île Clipperton. *L'Illustration*, Vol. 93, 1935, p. 39.

NETHERLANDS TERRITORIES
General

Atlas van Tropisch Nederland, uitgegeven door het Koninklijk Nederlandsch Aardrijkskundig Genootschap in samenwerking met den Topografischen Dienst in Nederlandsch-Indië. [Batavia], 1938.

Braak, C. Het klimaat van Nederlandsch West-Indië: The Climate of the Netherlands West Indies. (*Kon. Nederl. Meteorol. Inst., No. 102; Mededeelingen en verhandelingen 36.*) The Hague, [1935].

Encyclopaedie van Nederlandsch West-Indië, onder redactie van R. D. Benjamins en J. F. Snelleman. The Hague, 1914–1917.

Geschiedkundige atlas van Nederland: West-Indië door F. Oudschans Dentz en W. R. Menkman. The Hague, 1933.

Handbook of the Netherlands and overseas territories. The Hague, 1931.

Kielstra, J. C. Wirtschaftliche und soziale Probleme in Niederländisch-Westindien. (*Kieler Vorträge, 13*), Jena, 1925.

Territory of Curaçao

Bakker, H. B. The harbour of Curaçao. *Bull. Permanent Internatl. Assn. of Navigation Congresses*, 4th Year, 1929, pp. 80–88.

Balen, W. J. Van. Ons gebiedsdeel Curaçao. Haarlem, 1938.

Balen, W. J. Van. The Territory of Curaçao. *Bull. Colonial Inst. of Amsterdam*, Vol. 2, 1938–1939, pp. 115–121.

BALLOU, H. A. The Dutch Leeward Islands. *Tropical Agriculture*, Vol. 11, 1934, pp. 317–320.

Curaçao nummer. *Natuur en Mensch*, Vol. 54, Nos. 4–5, April—Mei, 1934.

Curaçaosch Verslag [1938], Vols. 1 and 2. The Hague. (Annual.)

Curaçao, transshipment port for north coast products. *Commerce Repts.*, No. 33, August 15, 1927, pp. 387–389.

DUNBAR, E. U. What oil did to Curaçao. *Journ. of Geogr.*, Vol. 33, 1934, pp. 340–345.

KNAPPERT, L. Geschiedenis van de Nederlandsche Bovenwindsche Eilanden in de 18de eeuw. *West-Indische Gids*, Vols. 11, 12, 13, 1929–1933.

PLATT, R. S. A Curaçao farmstead. *Journ. of Geogr.*, Vol. 35, 1936, pp. 154–156.

OUDSCHANS DENTZ, FRED. De opkomst van Curaçao. *West-Indische Gids*, Vol. 8, 1926, pp. 357–369.

RUTTEN, L. M. R. De geologische geschiedenis der drie Nederlandsche Benedenwindsche Eilanden. *West-Indische Gids*, Vol. 13, 1932, pp. 401–441.

U. S. Bur. of Foreign and Domestic Commerce. Markets of the Dutch West Indies, by H. P. Macgowan. (*Trade Information Bull. No. 405*), Washington, 1926.

VANDENBOSCH, AMRY. Dutch problems in the West Indies. *Foreign Affairs*, Vol. 9, 1930–1931, pp. 350–352.

WESTERMANN, J. H. The geology of Aruba. (*Geographische en geologische mededeelingen. Publicaties uit het Geographisch en uit het Mineralogisch-Geologisch Instituut der Rijks-Universiteit te Utrecht. Physiographisch-geologische Reeks No. 7.*) Utrecht, 1932.

West Indië nummer. *Economisch-Statistische Berichten*. 23e Jaargang, 4 Mei, 1938.

WINKLER, OTTO. Neiderländisch-Westindien: eine länderkundliche Skizze. *Mitt. Gesell. für Erdkunde zu Leipzig, 1923–1925*, 1926, pp. 87–137.

Territory of Surinam

CALOR, A. T. Beknopte aardrijkskunde van Suriname. Amsterdam, 1936.

IJZERMAN, R. Outline of the geology and petrology of Surinam (Dutch Guiana). The Hague, 1931.

Surinamsch Verslag [1938]. Vols. 1 and 2. The Hague. (Annual.)

VERKADE-CARTIER VAN DISSEL, E. F. De mogelijkheid van landbouw-kilonisatie voor blanken in Suriname. Amsterdam, 1937.

WARDLAW, C. W. Agriculture in Suriname. *Tropical Agriculture*, Vol. 7, 1930, pp. 31–37.

ISLAND TERRITORIES OF VENEZUELA AND COLOMBIA

Venezuelan Islands

AGUERREVERE, S. E. and V. M. LÓPEZ, Geología de la Isla del Gran Roque y sus depósitos de fosfatos. *Bol. Soc. Venezolana de Cienc. Nat.*, Vol. 5, 1939, pp. 137–172.

BÜRGER, OTTO. Venezuela, ein Führer durch das Land und seine Wirtschaft. Leipzig, 1922.

DALTON, L. V. Venezuela. London, 1912.

DE BOOY, THEODOOR. Island of Margarita, Venezuela. *Bull. Pan American Union*, Vol. 42, 1916, pp. 531–546.

HUMMELINCK, P. W. Apuntaciones sobre las aguas superficiales del Estado Nueva Esparta y dependencias federales. *Bol. Soc. Venezolana de Cienc. Nat.*, Vol. 5, 1939, pp. 173–178.

JOHNSTON, J. R. Flora of the islands of Margarita and Coche, Venezuela. *Contributions Gray Herbarium of Harvard Univ.*, No. 37, 1909; *Proc. Boston Soc. of Nat. Hist.*, Vol. 34, pp. 163–312.

LIDDLE, R. A. The geology of Venezuela and Trinidad. Fort Worth, [1928].

LOWE, P. R. A naturalist on desert islands. London, 1911.

RUTTEN, L. On rocks from the Venezuelan islands between Bonaire and Trinidad and on some rocks from northwestern Venezuela. *Kon. Akad. van Wetenschappen te Amsterdam, Proc. Sect. of Sciences*, Vol. 34, 1931, pp. 1101–1115.

SIEVERS, W. Die Inseln vor der Nordküste von Venezuela, *Globus*, Vol. 74, 1898, pp. 163–165, 291–294, 302–307.

Venezuela, Ministerio de fomento. Resumen general del sexto censo de población, 26 de diciembre de 1936. Carácas, 1938.

VILLEGAS RUIZ, J. DE D. Compendio de geografía física y política de Venezuela. 4th ed. Carácas, [1894].

Colombian Islands

Colombia. Direccion General de Estadistíca, Departamento de Contraloría. Censo de población de la República de Colombia levantado el 14 de octubre de 1918 y aprobado el 19 de septiembre de 1921 . . . Bogotá, 1924.

Colombia. Minist. de Relaciones Exteriores. *Boletin*, Vol. 1, Nos. 3-5. Bogotá, 1931.

Colombia Yearbook. [1935]. Edited by Abraham Martinez. Vol. 7. New York.

Informe que la Contraloría General de la República rinde al Sr. Ministro de Gobierno . . . sobre el levantamiento del Censo civil de 1938. *Anal. de Economía y Estadistíca*, Vol. 2, No. 4, Bogotá, 1939.

LÉVINE, V. Colombia; physical features, natural resources, means of communication, manufactures, and industrial development. New York, 1914.

MORA ANGUEIRA, HERNANDO. Archipiélago de San Andrés y Providencia. *Bol. Geogr. de Colombia*, Vol. 6, 1940, pp. 237-249.

U. S. Bur. of Foreign and Domestic Commerce. Colombia, a commercial and industrial handbook, by P. L. Bell. (*Special Agents Series No. 206*), Washington, 1921.

VERGARA Y VELASCA, F. J. Nueva geografía de Colombia. Vol. 1, Bogotá, 1901.

INDEX

This index does not cover the List of References (pp. 101–106). It is intended to provide a key to passages in the text where substantial information is given about the items indexed rather than to all casual references. The reader should also consult the analytical table of contents (pp. iii–iv).

Abbreviations: Barb., Barbadoes; *B.I.*, Bahama Islands; *Br. Gui.*, British Guiana; *Br. Hon.*, British Honduras; *Br. pos.*, British Caribbean possessions; *Cur.*, Territory of Curaçao; *Fr. Gui.*, French Guiana; *Guad.*, Guadeloupe and Dependencies; *J.*, Jamaica; *L.I.*, British Leeward Islands; *Mar.* Martinique; *N. Esp.*, Nueva Esparta; *S. And.* Intendencia of San Andrés and Providencia; *Sur.*, Surinam; *Tob.*, Tobago; *Trin.*, Trinidad; *W.I.*, British Windward Islands.